SHERLOCK HOLMES
CASE-BOOK OF
CURIOUS PUZZLES

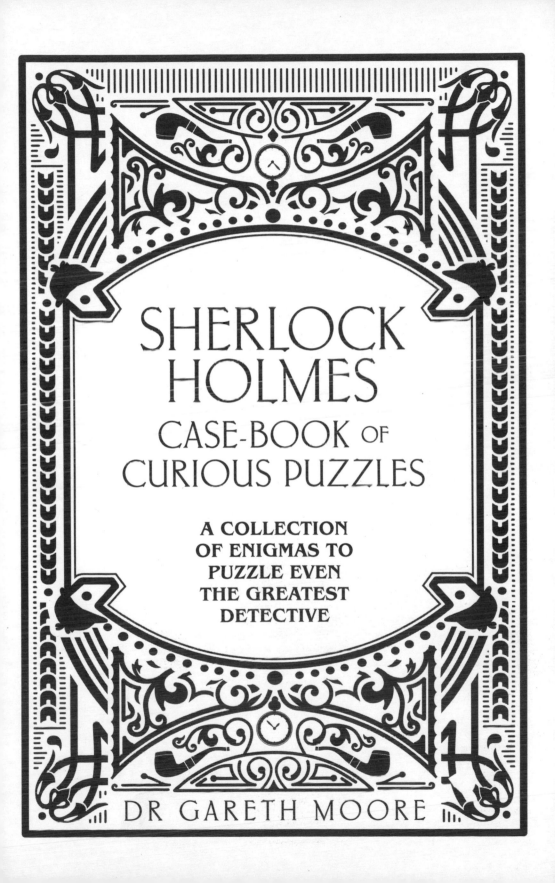

SHERLOCK HOLMES
CASE-BOOK OF
CURIOUS PUZZLES

**A COLLECTION
OF ENIGMAS TO
PUZZLE EVEN
THE GREATEST
DETECTIVE**

DR GARETH MOORE

CONTENTS

INTRODUCTION

Dear Reader,

Welcome to this most portentous volume. It is the very first of its
kind, for within the pages of this book I have collected together the
most unique puzzle vignettes. All have been gathered during the past
few years of my life, during which I have had the rare privilege to
accompany that most singular of detectives, Sherlock Holmes, on many
of his most renowned cases.

Should you somehow fail to have heard of the detective tour de force
that is Mr Sherlock Holmes, let me take a moment to introduce you to
him, peccadillos and all.

His signature feature is his towering intellect. His cranial
cogitations are majestic in their profundity, often reducing mere
mortals such as you, no doubt—and certainly I—to mere observers,
no matter how much we might wish to offer some additional insight
into his investigatory activities. Having already solved a mystery,
he enjoys playing with others in the way that a cat will tease its prey,
ensuring that you are never in any doubt as to how superior his own
intelligence is to yours. He will frequently challenge you to reach some
conclusion or the other, but it is invariably one that he has long ago
passed at the wayside in his own insatiable quest
for knowledge.

This book collects together more than 130 such challenges that
Holmes has set me over recent years, and which I present here in
written form for your edification and entertainment.

These challenges are of several different types. Some rely on
principles of the mathematical kind, while many need one or more
logical deductions to be made from the presented writings. A few make
reference to contemporary technology or other new inventions of our
Victorian era, and others require abstract thinking to explain some
apparently impossible situation. Let me assure you, however, that none
require any special knowledge or experience, beyond the wit that God
himself gave you as you entered this mortal world.

Holmes is rather fond of riddles, so I should also take this
opportunity to give you fair warning that at least a few of the challenges
require cleverness of the language variety, with a few plays on words
and the like. If a puzzle seems unsolvable, it is always worth considering

that some cleverness is at play and all is not as it seems. I have also seen fit to put a small hint into some of the puzzle titles, so if you should ever find yourself stuck it is always worth considering the true meaning of the title. It might perchance be of some small assistance in your hunt for even the most elusive of answers.

Should any of the conundrums herein happen to challenge and perplex you beyond your ken, I have (much against Holmes's recommendation, I might add) included full solutions at the back of this volume. Here I have stated the answer as it was originally given to me. This section might, I suggest, be given to a friend or detective colleague to read, so that they can concoct a hint that is slightly less fiendish than those already given to you on the puzzle pages.

Each challenge may be tackled on its own, and you may dip in and out of the book at your leisure. The material tells no grand overall story, beyond documenting the genius of the man I am lucky to call my friend: Mr Sherlock Holmes.

Doctor John Watson,
221B Baker Street, London, 1897

THE FIRST DEDUCTION

Holmes and I met with some of the Baker Street Irregulars to discuss a case. Before we arrived at the meeting place, he remarked that we were meeting with three boys who had worked with us before: Tom, Mickey, and Joe. The names rang bells, but I could not immediately remember which was which.

"Which cases did they help us with again, Holmes?" I asked, hoping that this would jog my memory.

"Oh, let me see, Watson. It was—if I remember your case names correctly—The Crimson Consideration, The Mark of Three, and The Case of the Vanishing Glass."

This helped me a little, and I recalled a connection between The Mark of Three and the name Joe. But I still could not picture him, and as for the remaining two boys, I had no idea which cases they had assisted us with.

When we arrived at our meeting, I realized that I did indeed recognize all three boys. One had a mole on his chin, another a scar beneath his eye, and the third had wild, bushy hair that sprang out from his head at all angles. I was confident that the one with the scar was Mickey, as I remembered a story about his brother giving him the scar in a fight. It was then that I remembered his impressive bushy hair had featured heavily in my account of The Case of the Vanishing Glass.

From these somewhat paltry recollections, I am pleased to say I was able to greet each boy by the correct name, and make some polite remark about the case he had helped us with.

Can you deduce which name belonged to which boy, and on which case he worked?

THE REIGATE SQUIRES

An original short story by Sir Arthur Conan Doyle

It was some time before the health of my friend Mr Sherlock Holmes recovered from the strain caused by his immense exertions in the spring of 1887. The whole question of the Netherland-Sumatra Company and of the colossal schemes of Baron Maupertuis are too recent in the minds of the public, and are too intimately concerned with politics and finance to be fitting subjects for this series of sketches. They led, however, in an indirect fashion to a singular and complex problem which gave my friend an opportunity of demonstrating the value of a fresh weapon among the many with which he waged his life-long battle against crime.

On referring to my notes I see that it was upon the 14th of April that I received a telegram from Lyons which informed me that Holmes was lying ill in the Hotel Dulong. Within twenty-four hours I was in his sick-room, and was relieved to find that there was nothing formidable in his symptoms. Even his iron constitution, however, had broken down under the strain of an investigation which had extended over two months, during which period he had never worked less than fifteen hours a day, and had more than once, as he assured me, kept to his task for five days at a stretch. Even the triumphant issue of his labours could not save him from reaction after so terrible an exertion, and at a time when Europe was ringing with his name and when his room was literally ankle-deep with congratulatory telegrams I found him a prey to the blackest depression. Even the knowledge that he had succeeded where the police of three countries had failed, and that he had outmanoeuvred at every point the most accomplished swindler in Europe, was insufficient to rouse him from his nervous prostration.

Three days later we were back in Baker Street together; but it was evident that my friend would be much the better for a change, and the thought of a week of spring time in the country was full of attractions to me also. My old friend, Colonel Hayter, who had come under my professional care in Afghanistan, had now taken a house near Reigate in Surrey, and had frequently asked me to come down to him upon a visit. On the last occasion he had remarked that if my friend would only come with me he would be glad to extend his hospitality to him also. A little diplomacy was needed, but when Holmes understood that the establishment was a bachelor one, and that he would be allowed the fullest freedom, he fell in with my plans and a week after our return from Lyons we were under the colonel's roof. Hayter was a fine old soldier who had seen much of the world, and he soon found, as I had expected, that Holmes and he had much in common.

On the evening of our arrival we were sitting in the colonel's gun-room after dinner, Holmes stretched upon the sofa, while Hayter and I looked over his little armoury of Eastern weapons.

"By the way," said he suddenly, "I think I'll take one of these pistols upstairs with me in case we have an alarm."

"An alarm!" said I.

"Yes, we've had a scare in this part lately. Old Acton, who is one of our county magnates, had his house broken into last Monday. No great damage done, but the fellows are still at large."

"No clue?" asked Holmes, cocking his eye at the colonel.

"None as yet. But the affair is a petty one, one of our little country crimes, which must seem too small for your attention, Mr Holmes, after this great international affair."

Holmes waved away the compliment, though his smile showed that it had pleased him.

"Was there any feature of interest?"

"I fancy not. The thieves ransacked the library and got very little for their pains. The whole place was turned upside down, drawers burst open, and presses ransacked, with the result that an odd volume of Pope's *Homer*, two plated candlesticks, an ivory letter-weight, a small oak barometer, and a ball of twine are all that have vanished."

"What an extraordinary assortment!" I exclaimed.

"Oh, the fellows evidently grabbed hold of everything they could get." Holmes grunted from the sofa.

"The county police ought to make something of that," said he; "why, it is surely obvious that—"

But I held up a warning finger.

the story continues on page 22

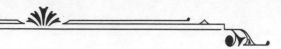

A SPECIAL NUMBER

Holmes once asked me, "Watson, do you have a preferred number?"

I thought about it for a moment, then answered, "I suppose I rather like three. It has something of a pleasing quality to it."

Holmes replied with a shake of his head, before proclaiming, "Where is your sense of adventure, Watson? Such a small number, and so little that can be said about it! Now tell me, what do you make of the number 8,549,176,320? It is a rather special one, if you ask me."

Indeed, it was. But why was it so special?

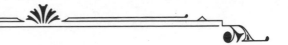

The Fast Train

A friend of mine works and lives in the city, but rather enjoys a jaunt to the countryside whenever possible. Each weekend, he heads off to King's Cross station around Saturday lunchtime and catches either the train to Leicester or the train to Dover, taking whichever is leaving first. Both run at perfect twenty minute intervals, but even though the exact time of his arrival at the station is random, he has found that around 90 per cent of the time he ends up in Leicester rather than Dover.

I reported this oddity to Holmes, who was of course immediately able to shed light on it.

What was the explanation?

The Case of the Red Widow

"Watson," asked Holmes, "did I ever tell you about the case of the Red Widow?"

"No," I answered, "but pray do."

"It was 1879, and I had not long been in the detective business when I heard that the Earl of Buckinghamshire had been plagued by the ghostly vision of a woman. He had seen her, framed in a doorway, wearing a glowing red dress—and then as he watched she melted away, fading ethereally into the whitewashed walls beyond."

"Goodness, Holmes," I exclaimed. "The man must have been mad. Both you and I know with perfect certainty that no inhabitant of the spectral realm has ever been proven to exist."

"I assure you, dear Watson, that the man was perfectly sane. What he had seen, however, was indeed not a ghost but rather a physical manifestation planted firmly within the terra firma of our own humble existence.

"If I were to continue and tell you that I later located the woman in entirely corporeal form, and that when the Earl had seen her she had been wearing a vivid, green dress on a bright, sunny day, can you venture an explanation as to what had truly transpired?"

THE IMPOSSIBLE BREAKFAST

Holmes and I were treating ourselves to a cooked breakfast at our preferred local eatery. As I was tucking into my Eggs Benedict, I noticed the waiter bring someone a dish that looked for all the world like chocolate ice cream.

"Really," I declaimed. "The things people have for breakfast! Some people will eat anything."

"Turns the stomach, does it not?" rejoined Holmes. "But of course, Watson, there are two things no one can ever eat for breakfast, no matter how strong their stomach."

What two things did he speak of?

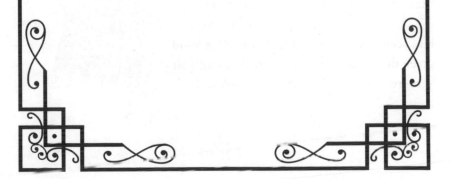

FOUR BY FOUR

"Here's an interesting little mathematical puzzle for you, Watson," said Holmes one day. "Can you find a way to make every whole number from 0 to 20 using exactly four 4s and whichever mathematical operations you wish?"

He gave me the example "$0 = \frac{4}{4} - \frac{4}{4}$" to start me off, but I then must admit it I rather struggled on some of the remaining numbers.

How well can you do, dear reader?

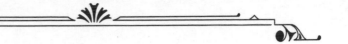

THE PRESENT-PACKING POSER

One year I had intended to ship some Yuletide presents to relatives of mine who were then living in the south of France. At the Baker Street Post Office, they informed me that the delivery would be charged by the number of shipping crates, but that each crate could carry 25 pounds. Now I happened to have precisely 75 pounds of goods, so naturally I wanted to use only three crates. My parcels were of the following weights: 1 pound, 2 pounds, 2 pounds (again), 4 pounds, 8 pounds, 9 pounds, 10 pounds, 11 pounds, 13 pounds and 15 pounds.

Did I manage to pack all of these parcels into three crates, without exceeding the weight limit of any one crate?

A MYSTERIOUS PLACE

Holmes and I were in Bedfordshire on a case. There had been a break-in at an old estate, and yet the muddy footprints found at the scene did not match any of the soil types in close proximity to the building. As a result, we went for an exploratory walk in the surrounding area, with Holmes bending down to pinch a little earth between his fingers every now and again.

Our journey was notable for its eerie quietude. We passed not a soul as we walked, and when we eventually reached the main road, there was not a vehicle in sight.

"It's like the land of the dead out here," I remarked.

"Watson," Holmes said, "you're a reasonably well-journeyed man, are you not?"

"Well yes, I suppose I am," I replied. "More so than your average London gentleman, I would venture."

"In that case, I am sure this is not the first time that you have come across a place that has roads without vehicles, streets without people, and rivers without a single living creature in them."

I scratched my head. "I can't say that I have, Holmes. Even in the quietest of places, there's always a person or two about, or a few tiddlers swimming in a stream."

But when he told me of the place he had in mind, I realized that of course I was familiar with it, and had in fact spent many a happy hour exploring its reaches. What was it?

GREAT NIECES AND GREAT NEPHEWS

"My niece Beatrice gave birth again last week," Mrs. Hudson announced one day. "And would you believe it? Another girl!"

Holmes and I exchanged a look. Mrs. Hudson had rather a large number of nephews and nieces, not to mention a rapidly expanding plethora of great nephews and great nieces, and it was becoming increasingly hard to keep track of who was who, or indeed who was whose.

"Indeed! How many children does Beatrice now have?" I asked.

"That's her fourth! And Agatha has three, but again all daughters and not a boy in sight. I do declare we need some kind of rule to stop them having any more girls until we've had some boys!"

I pondered this for a moment, before suggesting, "Perhaps there should be a general rule that once a family eventually has a boy, they must stop having children lest they later have a girl. That'll give the boys a chance to catch up."

Here, Holmes interjected. "But that would make not the slightest difference at all, Watson."

He was quite right, of course. Can you explain why?

The Reigate Squires continues from page 11

"You are here for a rest, my dear fellow. For Heaven's sake don't get started on a new problem when your nerves are all in shreds."

Holmes shrugged his shoulders with a glance of comic resignation towards the colonel, and the talk drifted away into less dangerous channels.

It was destined, however, that all my professional caution should be wasted, for next morning the problem obtruded itself upon us in such a way that it was impossible to ignore it, and our country visit took a turn which neither of us could have anticipated. We were at breakfast when the colonel's butler rushed in with all his propriety shaken out of him.

"Have you heard the news, sir?" he gasped. "At the Cunningham's sir!"

"Burglary!" cried the colonel, with his coffee-cup in mid-air.

"Murder!"

The colonel whistled. "By Jove!" said he. "Who's killed, then? The J.P. or his son?"

"Neither, sir. It was William the coachman. Shot through the heart, sir, and never spoke again."

"Who shot him, then?"

"The burglar, sir. He was off like a shot and got clean away. He'd just broke in at the pantry window when William came on him and met his end in saving his master's property."

"What time?"

"It was last night, sir, somewhere about twelve."

"Ah, then, we'll step over afterwards," said the colonel, coolly settling down to his breakfast again. "It's a baddish business," he added when the butler had gone; "he's our leading man about here, is old Cunningham, and a very decent fellow too. He'll be cut up over this, for the man has been in his service for years and was a good servant. It's evidently the same villains who broke into Acton's."

"And stole that very singular collection," said Holmes, thoughtfully.

"Precisely."

"Hum! It may prove the simplest matter in the world, but all the same at first glance this is just a little curious, is it not? A gang of burglars acting in the country might be expected to vary the scene of their operations, and not to crack two cribs in the same district within a few days. When you spoke last night of taking precautions I remember that it passed through my mind that this was probably the last parish in England to which the thief or thieves would be likely to turn their attention—which shows that I have still much to learn."

"I fancy it's some local practitioner," said the colonel. "In that case, of course, Acton's and Cunningham's are just the places he would go for, since they are far the largest about here."

"And richest?"

"Well, they ought to be, but they've had a lawsuit for some years which has sucked the blood out of both of them, I fancy. Old Acton has some claim on half Cunningham's estate, and the lawyers have been at it with both hands."

"If it's a local villain there should not be much difficulty in running him down," said Holmes with a yawn. "All right, Watson, I don't intend to meddle."

"Inspector Forrester, sir," said the butler, throwing open the door.

The official, a smart, keen-faced young fellow, stepped into the room. "Good-morning, Colonel," said he; "I hope I don't intrude, but we hear that Mr Holmes of Baker Street is here."

The colonel waved his hand towards my friend, and the inspector bowed.

"We thought that perhaps you would care to step across, Mr Holmes."

"The fates are against you, Watson," said he, laughing. "We were chatting about the matter when you came in, Inspector. Perhaps you can let us have a few details." As he leaned back in his chair in the familiar attitude I knew that the case was hopeless.

"We had no clue in the Acton affair. But here we have plenty to go on, and there's no doubt it is the same party in each case. The man was seen."

the story continues on page 34

The Barrel Quarrel

Holmes and I were having a quiet post-case drink at the local pub when we happened to overhear a disagreement between the landlord and a customer. The customer was buying what was left in a particular barrel of beer, and insisted that the barrel was less than half full and he should be charged accordingly. The landlord, meanwhile, maintained that it was more than half full and he wished to charge the customer accordingly. Fortunately for them, Holmes was able to help them resolve the question without using any measuring equipment.

How did he do it?

BROTHERS AND SISTERS

One day I asked our resident housekeeper, "Your nieces both have several children, do they not, Mrs. Hudson?"

"Oh, yes," she replied. "Beatrice has four daughters and no sons, but Agatha has only three daughters, although each of Agatha's daughters has one brother."

"So, Watson," quizzed Holmes, "which of them has the greater number of children?"

READING ROOM

As with his thoughts on so many things, Holmes' idea of a holiday is rather strange. The most recent example of this was last summer, when he decided that a rural stay in a basic wooden cabin was the luxury to which he truly aspired.

Upon his return, I asked him how he had enjoyed his sojourn.

"Most excellent," he replied. "The lack of so many of life's modern distractions allowed me to solve several historical cases that had been troubling me. With no running water, and no electric or gas lights, and indeed not even a proper bed, a mattress on the floor was all I needed to read through the case notes that I had brought with me."

"Goodness!" I rejoined. "So a fire was your only source of light? For reading your notes, I mean? Surely you strained your eyes?"

"But not at all. In fact, I had no ready means to light such a fire, even if I had wished to. The nights were quite hot enough without such an encumbrance."

If Holmes had no electricity or gas lighting, and no means of lighting a fire, how was he able to see well enough to read?

The Three Feet Feat

"I happened upon a three-legged donkey earlier today," I informed Holmes one afternoon. "The joke among us passers-by was that it was no longer a "donkey', but rather now a "wonky'."

"Very droll," Holmes remarked. "But I can do you one better. I saw something today with three feet and no legs. Can you tell me what it was?"

Indeed—what was it?

S. Rouyer

A FIRST KEYBOARD CONUNDRUM

"Watson," said Holmes, "you see that typewriter in the corner of the room? The one you use to write those fantastical reports of my detecting activities?"

"Why yes," I said, "although I say again that my reports do not in any way sensationalize your prodigious talents."

"Have you ever given thought to the longest word you could type with it?"

This seemed to me rather a bizarre question, until Holmes followed up shortly with: "What do you think the longest word you can type on the top row of that mechanical keyboard is? The one that reads QWERTYUIOP?"

And indeed, I pondered—what is the longest word I could type?

KEEPING UP WITH THE HUDSONS

"I discovered a rather remarkable thing about Mrs. Hudson's family the other day," Holmes observed.

"Her mother had a sixth finger?" I suggested.

"No, no, I've known about that for years," he replied. "I'm referring to the curious arrangement of her nieces and nephews. Mrs. Hudson's sister has four children, with a three-year age gap between each child and the next. Moreover, the oldest child is currently two-thirds of her mother's age, which is twice what the youngest child's age was last year."

"Well isn't that... something," I replied, somewhat disinterestedly.

"Indeed it is," said Holmes, failing, perhaps deliberately so, to note my lack of enthusiasm. "But tell me, Watson, from this information, can you deduce the age of Mrs. Hudson's sister?"

THE CUBOID CALENDAR

Early one January morning, I discovered that Holmes had not troubled himself with obtaining a new calendar for the new year. This was most inconvenient for me, as I like to keep a clear track of dates so that all my writings retain the correct chronology, for the best interests of my readers.

When I brought this to Holmes' attention, he went over to the basket of wood by the fireplace and picked out four large wooden cubes.

"Paint on these, Watson," he said, "and you'll be able to keep track of the date for ever more."

"Whatever do you mean?" I asked him.

He picked up a cube. "On this one you can write the names of the first six months, using one face for each month. On a second cube, you can write the other six. Then use the other two for numbers. Every day you can turn the cubes so that the appropriate date is visible, and that way you can keep track of the days."

This made some vague sense to me, so I set about painting the names of the months on the first two cubes. When I reached the second two, however, I hesitated, convinced that two cubes would not suffice for me to write enough numbers to be able to construct every number from 1 to 31.

Was it possible?

A CAREFULLY CONSTRUCTED NUMBER

"I came across a most pleasing number today, Watson," Holmes once said to me.

"I thought we had established by now that I do not share your capacity to find numbers pleasing," I replied. "They are merely prosaic representations of mathematical certitudes."

"Oh, my dear Watson, I am sure that in this instance you will surely make an exception. For there is a ten-digit number where the first digit is equal to the number of zeros in this magical number; the second digit is equal to the number of ones; the third reveals the number of twos there are; and so on, and so on, right up to the tenth digit, which reveals the number of nines there are."

"I must admit Holmes, that I do not believe such a number could exist. But should it be proven to so do, I would permit that it does indeed sound strangely satisfying."

Holmes was, of course, correct. But what is this mysterious number?

The Reigate Squires continues from page 23

"Ah!"

"Yes, sir. But he was off like a deer after the shot that killed poor William Kirwan was fired. Mr Cunningham saw him from the bedroom window, and Mr Alec Cunningham saw him from the back passage. It was quarter to twelve when the alarm broke out. Mr Cunningham had just got into bed, and Mr Alec was smoking a pipe in his dressing-gown. They both heard William the coachman calling for help, and Mr Alec ran down to see what was the matter. The back door was open, and as he came to the foot of the stairs he saw two men wrestling together outside. One of them fired a shot, the other dropped, and the murderer rushed across the garden and over the hedge. Mr Cunningham, looking out of his bedroom, saw the fellow as he gained the road, but lost sight of him at once. Mr Alec stopped to see if he could help the dying man, and so the villain got clean away. Beyond the fact that he was a middle-sized man and dressed in some dark stuff, we have no personal clue; but we are making energetic enquiries, and if he is a stranger we shall soon find him out."

"What was this William doing there? Did he say anything before he died?"

"Not a word. He lives at the lodge with his mother, and as he was a very faithful fellow we imagine that he walked up to the house with the intention of seeing that all was right there. Of course this Acton business has put everyone on their guard. The robber must have just burst open the door—the lock has been forced—when William came upon him."

"Did William say anything to his mother before going out?"

"She is very old and deaf, and we can get no information from her. The shock has made her half-witted, but I understand that she was never very bright. There is one very important circumstance, however. Look at this!"

He took a small piece of torn paper from a notebook and spread it out upon his knee.

"This was found between the finger and thumb of the dead man. It appears to be a fragment torn from a larger sheet. You will observe that the hour mentioned upon it is the very time at which the poor fellow met his fate. You see that his murderer might have torn the rest of the sheet from him or he might have taken this fragment from the murderer. It reads almost as though it were an appointment."

Holmes took up the scrap of paper, a facsimile of which is here reproduced.

at quarter to twelve

learn what

may be

"Presuming that it is an appointment," continued the inspector, "it is of course a conceivable theory that this William Kirwan—though he had the reputation of being an honest man, may have been in league with the thief. He may have met him there, may even have helped him to break in the door, and then they may have fallen out between themselves."

"This writing is of extraordinary interest," said Holmes, who had been examining it with intense concentration. "These are much deeper waters than I had thought." He sank his head upon his hands, while the inspector smiled at the effect which his case had had upon the famous London specialist.

"Your last remark," said Holmes, presently, "as to the possibility of there being an understanding between the burglar and the servant, and this being a note of appointment from one to the other, is an ingenious and not entirely impossible supposition. But this writing opens up—" He sank his head into his hands again and remained for some minutes in the deepest thought. When he raised his face again, I was surprised to see that his cheek was tinged with colour, and his eyes as bright as before his illness. He sprang to his feet with all his old energy.

the story continues on page 46

THE SECRET MESSAGE

While working on a case away from the metropolis of London, Holmes sent me a letter explaining that he believed he was being followed. He required me to send him a certain case file, but he insisted I send it in a locked box, in order to ensure it was not intercepted and read by his putative stalker. Now, it so happened that I had a padlock in the office with which I could lock the box, but I was the only one with the key and so could not get it to Holmes without the same risk of interception. Luckily, Holmes also possessed a padlock, but again he had the key and I did not.

How did Holmes expect me to get the message to him so that he could unlock it, but that no one else could?

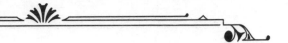

The Bamboozling Bacon

One day, Mrs. Hudson was cooking a rather fine breakfast when Holmes overheard her grumbling about the pan being too small.

"Watson," said Holmes, "why don't you help Mrs. Hudson maximize her bacon-frying efficiency?" He then called over to her to ask, "How long does it take to cook a rasher, Mrs. H?"

"I do a minute on each side," replied Mrs. Hudson. "But the pan only fits two rashers at once."

"Ah, but they are perfectly done every time," said Holmes, with one of his rare compliments that he only infrequently offered me. "So, Watson, what is the fastest way for Mrs. Hudson to fry three rashers (this being one rasher for each of us), without cutting any pieces in half?"

THE SECOND DEDUCTION

"This evening I shall be having two of my nieces and two of my great nieces over for tea," Mrs. Hudson told me one afternoon.

"Oh, how lovely, Mrs. Hudson. Which ones?" I asked, despite knowing perfectly well that even if she gave me their names this would in no way help me to recall exactly how they were all related.

"Jane, Margaret, Agatha, and Beatrice," she told me, as if with maternal pride.

"What a nice thing to be looking forward to," I said, making a mental note to be well away from Baker Street by the evening. "Do you have any plans for what you intend to do with them? Beyond having tea, I mean?"

"Well, I haven't seen Margaret and her sister in quite a while, so I'm looking forward to hearing all their news. And I've heard that Jane and her aunt had a little disagreement recently, so I'd be interested to hear about it from both sides. Naturally, Agatha will take her daughter's side. And of course Beatrice will tell everyone to listen to me, being the oldest and wisest of the group, but she's only saying that because she's older than the others and wants them to listen to her."

Can you deduce from this information how Jane, Margaret, Agatha, and Beatrice are related both to each other and to Mrs. Hudson?

THE PRIMARY SEQUENCE

It was around a year ago, while we were on a case over in Greenwich, that Holmes first began a rather irritating game. Whenever the mood struck him, he would begin a sequence of letters with an undisclosed theme, and would say nothing more to me until I had correctly told him the next letter in the sequence.

As I recall, the first sequence was as follows:

M, V, E, M, J, S, _

What did Holmes expect to come next, and why?

A Card Conundrum

During The Case of the Two of Hearts, Holmes and I were on the trail of a serial criminal who had committed a number of crimes in proximity to the establishment that called itself "The Flamin' Aces Casino". We felt sure that the crimes all had a single perpetrator because a calling card was found at the scene of each and every one—a two of hearts.

One evening, after Inspector Lestrade had shown us the stack of cards that the police had collected to date, Holmes turned to me with a question.

"Watson, do you have any interest in probability?"

"Not especially," I answered cautiously. "But why do you ask?"

"Cards always put me in mind of some interesting questions. For example, imagine that you draw two cards from a normal deck of all fifty-two cards. What is the probability that they are both twos, if I tell you that at least one is definitely a two?"

"Am I to take that example as purely illustrative?"

"Actually, no, Watson. Why don't you have a go at solving it?"

And so, with some reluctance, I did. What was the answer I eventually arrived at?

RED
AND GREEN APPLES

Holmes and I were at the Covent Garden market on an errand to obtain certain fruit and vegetables for Mrs. Hudson.

"Watson," Holmes said. "Here is a question of probability for you."

"Indeed?" I answered, somewhat reluctantly.

"Suppose I give you twenty green apples, twenty red apples, and two large sacks. I instruct you to divide the apples between the two bags in any way you like, using all of the apples. Once you have so done, I will blindfold you, shuffle the sacks, and you will be able to choose one sack and remove one apple. If the apple is red you will win some great reward, whereas if it is green you will bring some great punishment upon yourself. Given these rules, how do you divide the apples so as to maximize the chance that you will pick a red apple?"

Can you determine the best strategy?

EVEN MORE APPLES

Holmes was pleased with his apple-themed puzzle, so he decided to set me another.

"Now, imagine you have a sack of four apples. How can you divide those apples so that you can give one apple each to four people and yet still keep one in the sack?"

The Reigate Squires continues from page 35

"I'll tell you what," said he, "I should like to have a quiet little glance into the details of this case. There is something in it which fascinates me extremely. If you will permit me, Colonel, I will leave my friend Watson and you, and I will step round with the inspector to test the truth of one or two little fancies of mine. I will be with you again in half an hour."

An hour and half had elapsed before the inspector returned alone.

"Mr Holmes is walking up and down in the field outside," said he. "He wants us all four to go up to the house together."

"To Mr Cunningham's?"

"Yes, sir."

"What for?"

The inspector shrugged his shoulders. "I don't quite know, sir. Between ourselves, I think Mr Holmes had not quite got over his illness yet. He's been behaving very queerly, and he is very much excited."

"I don't think you need alarm yourself," said I. "I have usually found that there was method in his madness."

"Some folks might say there was madness in his method," muttered the inspector. "But he's all on fire to start, Colonel, so we had best go out if you are ready."

We found Holmes pacing up and down in the field, his chin sunk upon his breast, and his hands thrust into his trouser pockets.

"The matter grows in interest," said he. "Watson, your country-trip has been a distinct success. I have had a charming morning."

"You have been up to the scene of the crime, I understand," said the colonel.

"Yes; the inspector and I have made quite a little reconnaissance together."

"Any success?"

"Well, we have seen some very interesting things. I'll tell you what we did as we walk. First of all, we saw the body of this unfortunate man. He certainly died from a revolver wound as reported."

"Had you doubted it, then?"

"Oh, it is as well to test everything. Our inspection was not wasted. We then had an interview with Mr Cunningham and his son, who were able to point out the exact spot where the murderer had broken through the garden-hedge in his flight. That was of great interest."

"Naturally."

"Then we had a look at this poor fellow's mother. We could get no information from her, however, as she is very old and feeble."

"And what is the result of your investigations?"

"The conviction that the crime is a very peculiar one. Perhaps our visit now may do something to make it less obscure. I think that we are both agreed, Inspector, that the fragment of paper in the dead man's hand, bearing, as it does, the very hour of his death written upon it, is of extreme importance."

"It should give a clue, Mr Holmes."

"It does give a clue. Whoever wrote that note was the man who brought William Kirwan out of his bed at that hour. But where is the rest of that sheet of paper?"

"I examined the ground carefully in the hope of finding it," said the inspector.

"It was torn out of the dead man's hand. Why was someone so anxious to get possession of it? Because it incriminated him. And what would he do with it? Thrust it into his pocket, most likely, never noticing that a corner of it had been left in the grip of the corpse. If we could get the rest of that sheet it is obvious that we should have gone a long way towards solving the mystery."

"Yes, but how can we get at the criminal's pocket before we catch the criminal?"

"Well, well, it was worth thinking over. Then there is another obvious point. The note was sent to William. The man who wrote it could not have taken it; otherwise, of course, he might have delivered his own message by word of mouth. Who brought the note, then? Or did it come through the post?"

the story continues on page 58

THE LONG WALK

"I saw a former associate of mine last week," Holmes told me. "He is an American, but is spending a month's holiday in France."

"He's a lucky man to have such a lengthy holiday!" I replied. "Where in America is he from?"

"Texas," he replied. "And in fact, he told me a rather interesting thing. He happened to mention that he had journeyed to Paris from his home in Austin in just over a week, almost entirely on foot. Does that not sound the most remarkable feat, Watson?"

"It sounds remarkably false, I should say. No man is capable of such speed, Holmes."

"You are far too quick to throw around such assertions of impossibility, Watson, as I have told you on many previous occasions. Indeed, I tell you it is not impossible, and I quite believe that he was telling the truth."

How was this feat possible?

Clipped Wings

Holmes and I were taking a stroll outdoors when a pigeon flew abruptly across our path, causing me to duck.

"Infernal beasts," I said. "Why must our city be so plagued with these flying rats?"

Holmes demurred on my assessment, but then remarked, "This reminds me of an interesting point, Watson," before continuing, "No doubt you are familiar with the phenomenon of flightless birds?"

"Well yes of course," I replied. "The ostrich, the emu and the irrepressible penguin, and not to mention the long-lost dodo. A rather sad state of affairs to have wings which will never fly."

"On that I quite agree," said Holmes. "But can you name an animal which has no wings and yet will one day fly?" He made clear he was not referring to any kind of assisted flight, with hot air balloons or the like.

THE FIRST REBUS

Holmes and I were investigating a doctor, in relation to a strange series of poisonings that had been going on in North London. The man was absent when we called by his office, so we took the opportunity to look around the premises. We observed that he had made notes next to the names of some of his patients, and one of them read as follows:

I drew this to the attention of Holmes as a subject of possible suspicion.

"I'm afraid I don't think this is going to be much use to us, Watson," was all he offered.

What did the doctor's note say?

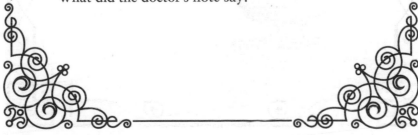

THE IMPATIENT POCKET WATCH

Holmes and I were walking through the great city of London on our way to a meeting with a prospective client. We had agreed to meet him in the early afternoon at half past one, having set out for our walk at about one o'clock.

"What time is it, Watson?" Holmes asked me.

I pulled out my pocket watch.

"It's…", I began, before following up this grand pronouncement a short moment later with, "Oh!".

"Whatever is the matter, Watson? I will not believe you if you tell me we are running late."

"No—well, actually I am not sure. I had forgotten that my pocket watch has started gaining five minutes for every hour that passes. Look—now it says that the time is six minutes past three."

"And when did you last set it, Watson?"

"It was at five o'clock yesterday evening. I remember hearing the bell ring as I entered 221B Baker Street, and thinking that I must reset it right away."

"Well from that information we can work out the time easily enough."

What time was it?

CELEBRITY CONUNDRUM

"Watson," Holmes said to me one day, "You like to keep in touch with the news, do you not? You are a fickle follower of fame and celebrity, and all that tittle and tattle from the society pages?"

"I suppose I do have a certain interest in the lives of others," I replied cautiously, before adding, "And I might point out that you have occasionally seen the benefit of my knowledge of society."

"Here's a little puzzle you might enjoy, then," he announced, before continuing with great pomp: "William Gladstone has a long one. Alexander Graham Bell has a short one. Queen Victoria doesn't have one. Casanova always used his. The Pope never uses his."

What was Holmes referring to?

The Third Deduction

I usually keep my notes in case files that live in the drawers of a now rather full filing cabinet, but recently I had cause to keep a couple of them out on my desk in anticipation of writing one of my well-received reports. Unfortunately, Holmes had left the window open and then gone out, and so when I returned home I found the various pieces of paper in a state of disarray, strewn across the floor. This was most frustrating, as the cases had taken place long enough ago that I was unable to entirely remember the details of each one. What I was, however, able to gather from the loose pieces of paper was as follows:

The three cases were to be entitled The Adventure of the Broken Table, The Adventure of the Frozen Lake, and The Adventure of the Moving Statue.

There were three victims, called John Bell, Sarah Doyle, and Mark Robinson.

There were three perpetrators, called Juliet Lane, Charlotte Green, and Peter Watkins.

The crimes committed were robbery, fraud, and murder.

Moreover, between the two of us, Holmes and I were able to remember a few key facts about the cases:

Juliet Lane defrauded her uncle.

Mark Robinson's body was found under a lake that had frozen over.

Peter Watkins was caught because of a splinter in his hand which he'd obtained from the jagged edge of a dining room table at the crime scene.

Combining these facts together, we were able to deduce the victim, perpetrator and crime committed in each of the three cases. Can you do the same?

The Reigate Squires continues from page 47

"I have made enquiries," said the inspector. "William received a letter by the afternoon post yesterday. The envelope was destroyed by him."

"Excellent!" cried Holmes, clapping the inspector on the back. "You've seen the postman. It is a pleasure to work with you. Well, here is the lodge, and if you will come up, Colonel, I will show you the scene of the crime."

We passed the pretty cottage where the murdered man had lived, and walked up an oak-lined avenue to the fine old Queen Anne house, which bears the date of Malplaquet upon the lintel of the door. Holmes and the inspector led us round it until we came to the side gate, which is separated by a stretch of garden from the hedge which lines the road. A constable was standing at the kitchen door.

"Throw the door open, officer," said Holmes. "Now, it was on those stairs that young Mr Cunningham stood and saw the two men struggling just where we are. Old Mr Cunningham was at that window—the second on the left—and he saw the fellow get away just to the left of that bush. Then Mr Alec ran out and knelt beside the wounded man. The ground is very hard, you see, and there are no marks to guide us." As he spoke two men came down the garden path, from round the angle of the house. The one was an elderly man, with a strong, deep-lined, heavy-eyed face; the other a dashing young fellow, whose bright, smiling expression and showy dress were in strange contract with the business which had brought us there.

"Still at it, then?" said he to Holmes. "I thought you Londoners were never at fault. You don't seem to be so very quick, after all."

"Ah, you must give us a little time," said Holmes good-humouredly.

"You'll want it," said young Alec Cunningham. "Why, I don't see that we have any clue at all."

"There's only one," answered the inspector. "We thought that if we could only find—Good heavens, Mr Holmes! What is the matter?"

My poor friend's face had suddenly assumed the most dreadful expression. His eyes rolled upwards, his features writhed in agony, and with a suppressed groan he dropped on his face upon the ground. Horrified at the suddenness and severity of the attack, we carried him into the kitchen, where he lay back in a large chair, and breathed heavily for some minutes. Finally, with a shamefaced apology for his weakness, he rose once more.

"Watson would tell you that I have only just recovered from a severe illness," he explained. "I am liable to these sudden nervous attacks."

"Shall I send you home in my trap?" asked old Cunningham.

"Well, since I am here, there is one point on which I should like to feel sure. We can very easily verify it."

"What was it?"

"Well, it seems to me that it is just possible that the arrival of this poor fellow William was not before, but after, the entrance of the burglar into the house. You appear to take it for granted that, although the door was forced, the robber never got in."

"I fancy that is quite obvious," said Mr Cunningham, gravely. "Why, my son Alec had not yet gone to bed, and he would certainly have heard anyone moving about."

"Where was he sitting?"

"I was smoking in my dressing-room."

"Which window is that?"

"The last on the left next to my father's."

"Both of your lamps were lit, of course?"

"Undoubtedly."

"There are some very singular points here," said Holmes, smiling. "Is it not extraordinary that a burglar—and a burglar who had had some previous experience—should deliberately break into a house at a time when he could see from the lights that two of the family were still afoot?"

"He must have been a cool hand."

"Well, of course, if the case were not an odd one we should not have been driven to ask you for an explanation," said young Mr Alec. "But as to your ideas that the man had robbed the house before William tackled him, I think it a most absurd notion. Wouldn't we have found the place disarranged, and missed the things which he had taken?"

the story continues on page 70

LOST AND FOUND

I recently lost my keys to the front door of 221B Baker Street, and spent several hours turning our chambers upside down looking for them. Finally, when they were fully upside down, it occurred to me that perhaps I might have left them in the kitchen when I went to greet Mrs. Hudson upon arriving home the previous day. And, of course, there they were indeed, plain for all to see.

"Why is it," I said to Holmes irritably, "that whenever you lose something, it's always in the very last place you look?"

"Well I should think there's a perfectly good reason for that, Watson."

What reason did Holmes have in mind?

THE SECOND KEYBOARD CONUNDRUM

"Back at the old typewriter again, Watson?" Holmes asked me, as I sat recording our latest case.

"It is my most faithful companion," I responded, before acerbically adding, "and somewhat more reliable than you I might add!"

Holmes ignored the barb, saying, "Yes, yes. Let's resume where we left off, then, shall we? What do you think is the longest word you can type with only the middle row of that keyboard? The one that reads ASDFGHJKL?"

CROSSING THE BRIDGE

I do not recall if I have mentioned before that I am not a particular fan of heights, but it is true. You can perhaps begin to imagine my horror, then, when I discovered that in order to reach a particular client we were required to walk across a rickety old rope bridge across a deep crevasse— and at night, with only one torch between us!

To his credit, Holmes did notice my discomfort and try to take my mind off it, but unfortunately his proposed method of distraction did nothing to make me feel better.

"Consider this, Watson," he said. "The two of us and two others—let us say Mrs. Hudson and Inspector Lestrade—are attempting to cross a bridge at night, with just a single torch between us. The bridge is a little unstable, so only two of us can be on the bridge at any one time, and none of us is willing to cross without the torch."

"I'm not sure that considering this is going to help me, Holmes."

"Nonsense," he replied. "We have not arrived at the crux of the matter. So, let us say that it takes me one minute to cross in either direction, being physically fit and not particularly fearful. Lestrade takes two minutes to cross in either direction. You, being somewhat more, shall we say, cautious, take five minutes to cross. And dear Mrs. Hudson, being both a little nervous and not in her physical prime, takes ten minutes to cross. What is the shortest time in which the four of us can all cross from one side to the other, bearing in mind that the torch will need to be taken back each time?"

JUGGLING JUICES

Mrs. Hudson was hosting a tea party for her extended family, and she had somewhat optimistically placed Holmes in charge of giving out the food she had prepared while I served the drinks. As I boiled water to make the many cups of tea that this activity required, and tried desperately to locate enough teacups for the entire party, I observed Holmes perfunctorily tip the snacks and finger sandwiches Mrs. Hudson had prepared onto a plate that was far too small for them, deposit it dramatically on the table in front of the guests and then swing out of the room with the air of one who has suffered the greatest of indignities.

When I had finally delivered as many cups of tea as there were guests, Mrs. Hudson announced that in fact since six of the guests were children they should have fruit juice rather than tea. Attempting not to display any irritation due to all of the unnecessary tea I had brewed, I found the bottle of juice that Mrs. Hudson had directed me to, located six glasses and began pouring—but unfortunately I managed to finish the entire bottle after filling just three of the glasses.

Holmes, who had returned and was now standing around with the air of one who had recently achieved saintliness, came over and found me staring at the row of six glasses, the first three of which were filled and the last three of which stood forlorn and empty.

"Watson," he said, "you have only filled the first three glasses."

"Yes," I replied tersely, "I am well aware of that."

"By touching only one glass, how can you make it so that your row alternates between full and empty glasses?"

How could it be done?

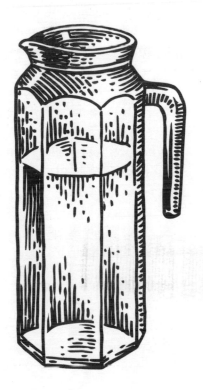

Cake Conundrum

At the tea party I wrote about on the preceding pages, the four youngest children were all very keen to eat as many slices of cake as possible, and so to make sure there were some left for everyone else I designated one plate of cake specifically for them (having first cleaned up the mess that Holmes had made of serving the edibles).

When the first child came to get his share, he took half of the slices of cake on the plate, plus an extra slice.

When the second child came to get her share, she took half of the remaining cake from the plate, and, again, took an extra one slice.

When the third child came to get his share, he too took half of the remaining cake plus one piece.

When the fourth child's turn came, there was no cake left, and she promptly burst into tears and had to be given a slice from another plate.

So how many slices of cake were there on the children's plate to begin with?

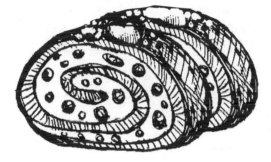

A CODED MESSAGE

One occupational hazard of the detective business is the paranoid client who is certain his every move is being watched. As a corollary of this, Holmes and I have received a rather large number of coded communications over the years, which it amuses Holmes to make me decipher.

The first that I shall recount to you read as follows:

CO
MET OFIF
TEE NJUN
IPE RSTRE
ET

What did it say?

THE MIXED-UP LABEL

Mrs. Hudson had a rather large number of her extended family over for tea, and during this time a particularly mischievous great nephew took the opportunity to wreak havoc in the kitchen. Seeing that the salt and sugar were kept in identical jars, he managed to find another identical jar in her extensive cupboards and poured alternating layers of salt and sugar into it. The young beast then removed the labels from the existing salt and sugar jars. When his tomfoolery was later discovered, he agreed to reattach the salt and sugar labels, and even helpfully created a

third label that read "MIXED". We soon discovered, however, that he had in fact attached each and every label to the wrong jar.

Holmes was very amused by this little prank, and remarked to Mrs. Hudson that in order to rectify the situation she need only taste a single spoonful from one jar.

How could it be done?

69

The Reigate Squires continues from page 59

"It depends on what the things were," said Holmes. "You must remember that we are dealing with a burglar who is a very peculiar fellow, and who appears to work on lines of his own. Look, for example, at the queer lot of things which he took from Acton's—what was it?—a ball of string, a letter-weight, and I don't know what other odds and ends."

"Well, we are quite in your hands, Mr Holmes," said old Cunningham. "Anything which you or the inspector may suggest will most certainly be done."

"In the first place," said Holmes, "I should like you to offer a reward—coming from yourself, for the officials may take a little time before they would agree upon the sum, and these things cannot be done too promptly. I have jotted down the form here, if you would not mind signing it. Fifty pounds was quite enough, I thought."

"I would willingly give five hundred," said the J.P., taking the slip of paper and the pencil which Holmes handed to him. "This is not quite correct, however," he added, glancing over the document.

"I wrote it rather hurriedly."

"You see you begin, 'Whereas, at about a quarter to one on Tuesday morning an attempt was made,' and so on. It was at a quarter to twelve, as a matter of fact."

I was pained at the mistake, for I knew how keenly Holmes would feel any slip of the kind. It was his specialty to be accurate as to fact, but his recent illness had shaken him, and this one little incident was enough to show me that he was still far from being himself. He was obviously embarrassed for an instant, while the inspector raised his eyebrows, and Alec Cunningham burst into a laugh. The old gentleman corrected the mistake, however, and handed the paper back to Holmes.

"Get it printed as soon as possible," he said; "I think your idea is an excellent one."

Holmes put the slip of paper carefully away into his pocket-book.

"And now," said he, "it really would be a good thing that we should all go over the house together and make certain that this rather erratic burglar did not, after all, carry anything away with him."

Before entering, Holmes made an examination of the door which had been forced. It was evident that a chisel or strong knife had been thrust in, and the lock forced back with it. We could see the marks in the wood where it had been pushed in.

"You don't use bars, then?" he asked.

"We have never found it necessary."

"You don't keep a dog?"

"Yes, but he is chained on the other side of the house."

"When do the servants go to bed?"

"About ten."

"I understand that William was usually in bed also at that hour."

"Yes."

"It is singular that on this particular night he should have been up. Now, I should be very glad if you would have the kindness to show us over the house, Mr Cunningham."

A stone-flagged passage, with the kitchens branching away from it, led by a wooden staircase directly to the first floor of the house. It came out upon the landing opposite to a second more ornamental stair which came up from the front hall. Out of this landing opened the drawing-room and several bedrooms, including those of Mr Cunningham and his son. Holmes walked slowly, taking keen note of the architecture of the house. I could tell from his expression that he was on a hot scent, and yet I could not in the least imagine in what direction his inferences were leading him.

"My good sir," said Mr Cunningham with some impatience, "this is surely very unnecessary. That is my room at the end of the stairs, and my son's is the one beyond it. I leave it to your judgement whether it was possible for the thief to have come up here without disturbing us."

"You must try round and get on a fresh scent, I fancy," said the son with a rather malicious smile.

the story continues on page 82

ANOTHER CARD CONUNDRUM

I came home to find Holmes absent-mindedly shuffling a deck of cards as he sat in his armchair. The sight of it filled me with a sudden dread, for I knew that some kind of infernal riddle was sure to follow.

"Ah, Watson," he said, without looking up as I came in. "I've been waiting for you."

"I presume you have some kind of pointless card puzzle to torture me with, do you?" I asked.

"Well, that wasn't my intent, but now that you mention it that does seem like rather good sport. So yes. Do you remember our little probability puzzle from last time?"

I sighed. "Yes. You asked me the probability of drawing two twos from a deck of cards, given that one draw was a two."

"Quite right, Watson. Now, here's a fun follow-up. What, would you say, is the probability of drawing two twos from a deck of cards, given that one draw was a two of hearts?"

"Surely the answer is no different from the first case, Holmes? How could it make a difference to know that one card was specifically a two of hearts, rather than just a two?"

"Well, you tell me, Watson."

Does it make a difference? And if so, how?

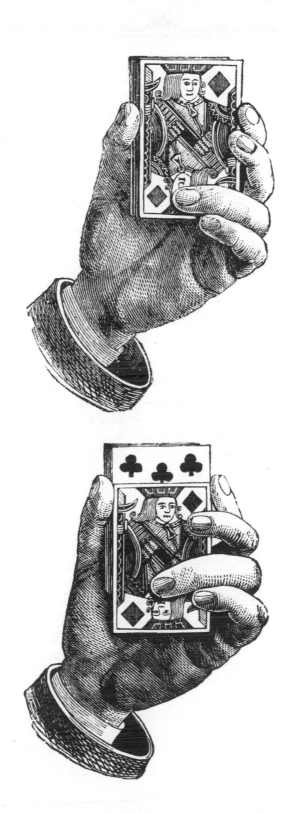

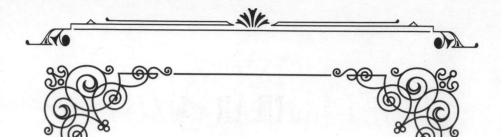

The Two Dentists

After an unfortunate incident with a rock cake at a village fête, I found myself in need of an emergency trip to the local dentist while deep in rural England. The small town I was staying in happened to have exactly two such practitioners, and what a remarkable difference between them: one man had a clean and orderly office that it was a pleasure to visit, and greeted me with a broad smile full of dazzling white teeth; while the other lived in a state of total disarray, and though his scowl rarely revealed much of his mouth I was able to discern that it was full of a number of ill-administered fillings.

"So naturally," I later explained to Holmes, "I intend to book an appointment with the former dentist."

"Good heavens, Watson!" Holmes exclaimed. "How could you make such a terrible blunder!"

Why did Holmes think I was making the wrong choice?

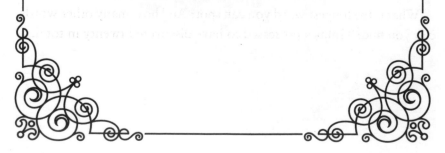

The Circular Puzzle

On most weekends Holmes and I find ourselves called away on business, so it is a rare Sunday morning that finds us both sitting and examining that day's papers. When this does happen, however, Holmes often calls out to mock any puzzles he finds among the pages, laughing at what he regards as the childish simplicity of their conundrums.

One morning, though, he summoned my attention away from a particularly fascinating article on a new animal discovered in the far throws of the Empire to show me a new type of puzzle being featured in the paper.

"Look at this circle of letters, Watson," he said. "It is a puzzle so simple that a child can understand it, so I thought you might enjoy it. The aim is to try and create as many words as you can, each of which uses the letter in the middle plus some combination of two or more others. In fact, I've already spotted a rather apt nine-letter one."

What is the longest word you can spot? And how many other words can you find? Holmes professed to have discovered twenty in total.

The Secondary Sequence

Not long after he had set me that first sequence conundrum, I was busy trying to schedule Holmes an appointment at the bank, when with no warning whatsoever he said:

"T, W, T, F, S."

At first I took him to be thinking out loud about a case, but it was only when he refused to elucidate any further that I realized he wanted me to again continue a sequence.

What letter ought I to have said next?

The Fourth Deduction

Holmes and I were investigating the theft of a priceless first-edition George Eliot novel from the archives of a local library. The man at the reception desk, however, was extremely old and, as we later discovered, had a rather poor memory of the day of the theft. He could tell us only that three men had visited the archives that day: Brian Pearson, Theodore McNab, and Nicholas Richardson. He knew this only because each visitor had written their names on a different entry form, and so there was no record of the order in which they had visited.

"And you have no recollection yourself of who was your first visitor of that day?" Holmes queried.

"Well, let me see…" The man scratched his chin. "I think the first man had rather a long first name, as when I wished him a good morning he told me to call him by some shortened version of it. I can't tell you what he looked like, though, I'm afraid— my spectacles were at home and my granddaughter, bless her, didn't bring them in for me until he had left."

"And do you remember anything else at all about that day, or any of these men?"

Holmes showed the man the list of the three names he had made.

"Well, let me see…" said the man, now scratching his head. "Nicholas Richardson. I liked him. He was dressed very smartly, you see, taking things seriously. Much better than this other man we'd had earlier in the day, who was dressed in overalls, would you believe? Hardly appropriate clothes for the archive, if you ask me."

"You thought this man in overalls was suspicious?"

"Oh, yes." The old man looked positively gleeful. "I had an intuition about him, Mr. Holmes. I thought to myself,

"He's not a man to be trusted.' That's why I stayed with him while he was in the archives, sir, to make sure the Eliot book was safe. It's our greatest treasure you know."

"Aha. Well, thank you very much for your help, sir," said Holmes. "I now know who stole the book, and I am sure it will be recovered soon."

Can you deduce, as Holmes did, which of the three men stole the book, and when he visited?

THE SAME TEA

While we were on a case in a distant part of the city, we partook of a late breakfast at a somewhat run-down café, where Holmes was rather annoyed to notice a fly in his tea. He summoned over the waiter and asked to be brought a new cup, at which the waiter took his tea and hurried off in the direction of the kitchens.

"Call me cynical, Watson, but I feel certain that fellow will simply remove the fly and then bring me back the same cup."

Shortly, the waiter returned with a fly-free cup of tea.

"I do apologise for the mishap, sir," he said, handing it to Holmes.

Holmes nodded in thanks, but moments after the waiter had left us he turned to me and shook his head. "I knew it. The very same tea. That waiter is as lazy as the café is unhygienic."

How did Holmes know it was the same cup of tea?

The Reigate Squires continues from page 71

"Still, I must ask you to humour me a little further. I should like, for example, to see how far the windows of the bedrooms command the front. This, I understand is your son's room"—he pushed open the door—"and that, I presume, is the dressing-room in which he sat smoking when the alarm was given. Where does the window of that look out to?" He stepped across the bedroom, pushed open the door, and glanced round the other chamber.

"I hope that you are satisfied now?" said Mr Cunningham, tartly.

"Thank you, I think I have seen all that I wished."

"Then if it is really necessary we can go into my room."

"If it is not too much trouble."

The J.P. shrugged his shoulders, and led the way into his own chamber, which was a plainly furnished and commonplace room. As we moved across it in the direction of the window, Holmes fell back until he and I were the last of the group. Near the foot of the bed stood a dish of oranges and a carafe of water. As we passed it Holmes, to my unutterable astonishment, leaned over in front of me and deliberately knocked the whole thing over. The glass smashed into a thousand pieces and the fruit rolled about into every corner of the room.

"You've done it now, Watson," said he, coolly. "A pretty mess you've made of the carpet."

I stooped in some confusion and began to pick up the fruit, understanding for some reason my companion desired me to take the blame upon myself. The others did the same, and set the table on its legs again.

"Hullo!" cried the inspector, "where's he got to?"

Holmes had disappeared.

"Wait here an instant," said young Alec Cunningham. "The fellow is off his head, in my opinion. Come with me, father, and see where he has got to!"

They rushed out of the room, leaving the inspector, the colonel, and me staring at each other.

"'Pon my word, I am inclined to agree with Master Alec," said the official. "It may be the effect of this illness, but it seems to me that—"

His words were cut short by a sudden scream of "Help! Help! Murder!" With a thrill I recognised the voice of that of my friend. I rushed madly from the room on to the landing. The cries, which had sunk down into a hoarse, inarticulate shouting, came from the room which we had first visited. I dashed in, and on into the dressing-room beyond. The two Cunninghams were bending over the prostrate figure of Sherlock Holmes, the younger clutching his throat with both hands, while the elder seemed to be twisting one of his wrists. In an instant the three of us had torn them away from him, and Holmes staggered to his feet, very pale and evidently greatly exhausted.

"Arrest these men, Inspector," he gasped.

"On what charge?"

"That of murdering their coachman, William Kirwan."

The inspector stared about him in bewilderment. "Oh, come now, Mr Holmes," said he at last, "I'm sure you don't really mean to—"

Never certainly have I seen a plainer confession of guilt upon human countenances. The older man seemed numbed and dazed with a heavy, sullen expression upon his strongly-marked face. The son, on the other hand, had dropped all that jaunty, dashing style which had characterized him, and the ferocity of a dangerous wild beast gleamed in his dark eyes and distorted his handsome features. The inspector said nothing, but, stepping to the door, he blew his whistle. Two of his constables came at the call.

"I have no alternative, Mr Cunningham," said he. "I trust that this may all prove to be an absurd mistake, but you can see that—Ah, would you? Drop it!" He struck out with his hand, and a revolver which the younger man was in the act of cocking clattered down upon the floor.

"Keep that," said Holmes, quietly putting his foot upon it; "you will find it useful at the trial. But this is what we really wanted." He held up a little crumpled piece of paper.

"The remainder of the sheet!" cried the inspector.

"Precisely."

"And where was it?"

the story continues on page 94

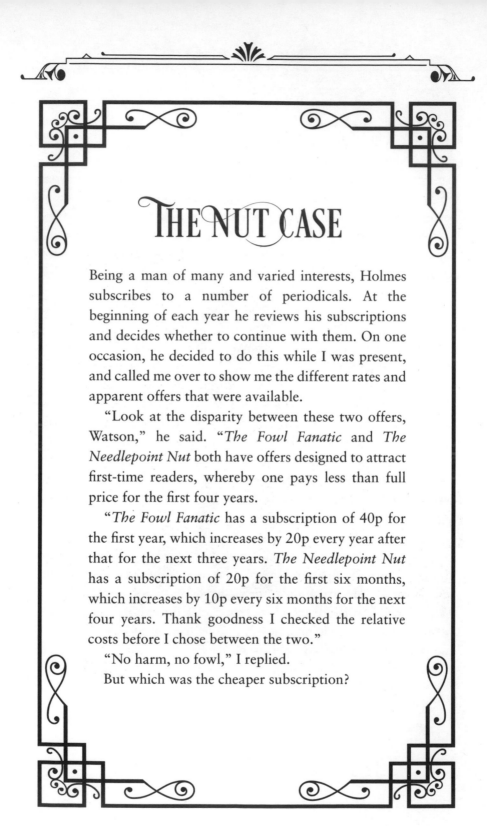

The Nut Case

Being a man of many and varied interests, Holmes subscribes to a number of periodicals. At the beginning of each year he reviews his subscriptions and decides whether to continue with them. On one occasion, he decided to do this while I was present, and called me over to show me the different rates and apparent offers that were available.

"Look at the disparity between these two offers, Watson," he said. "*The Fowl Fanatic* and *The Needlepoint Nut* both have offers designed to attract first-time readers, whereby one pays less than full price for the first four years.

"*The Fowl Fanatic* has a subscription of 40p for the first year, which increases by 20p every year after that for the next three years. *The Needlepoint Nut* has a subscription of 20p for the first six months, which increases by 10p every six months for the next four years. Thank goodness I checked the relative costs before I chose between the two."

"No harm, no fowl," I replied.

But which was the cheaper subscription?

A STRANGE GARDEN

"Watson," said Holmes one day, "I just came across a most curious garden. In one flowerbed, all except two of the flowers were roses; all except two were tulips; and all except two were geraniums."

"Can you tell me how many of each flower there were in the bed?"
How many indeed?

ℭOMMON PROPERTY

Recently I came across a scrap of paper with some words idly scrawled on it in Holmes' handwriting. The words were as follows:

Adopt

Begin

Biopsy

Deity

Empty

What common property do these words share which might have given Holmes cause to write them down?

THE FOUR COINS

Holmes had kindly loaned me some money while we were out one day. I was perturbed to discover upon arriving home that evening that my pockets had been picked and the cash was gone. A few days later, I attempted to return the borrowed amount, but Holmes stopped me.

"Watson, I'm quite happy for you to keep the money."

"That's very kind of you, Holmes, but quite unnecessary, I assure you," I replied.

"I shall make you a deal, then, Watson. I will let you keep the money on one condition." He continued, "Here. You are now holding four pennies in your hand. I will let you keep the original money if you are able to arrange those four pennies so that each one is touching all three of the others."

This task sounded easy enough, so I placed the four pennies flat on the table and pushed them all alongside one another. This was when it became apparent to me that things were more difficult than I had first anticipated, as it seemed impossible to make more than three of them touch at one time. I stared at the coins for quite a while before, finally, inspiration hit.

How did I pass Holmes' test?

HIGH TIME

Holmes and I were passing by the Houses of Parliament at midday, when we heard the familiar chime of the Clock Tower.

"Watson," Holmes said, "have you ever been curious as to the exact height of the Clock Tower?"

"Only mildly, but yes I suppose so," I replied.

Holmes answered with a riddle, as he so often did. "Well, then, it might interest you to know that it is approximately 70 yards plus one third of its total height tall."

How tall is the Clock Tower?

A SIBLING SUM

Mrs. Hudson had her extended family over once again for tea and, as I was in at the time, I decided I ought to try and make conversation.

The first guests I came across were a fairly young boy and girl who I took to be a great nephew and great niece of Mrs. Hudson.

"Are you two brother and sister?" I asked them.

They nodded.

"And have you any other siblings?"

"I've got the same number of brothers as sisters," the girl told me.

The boy frowned. "But I've got twice as many sisters as brothers."

How many siblings were there in the family?

A ONE-WAY ODDITY

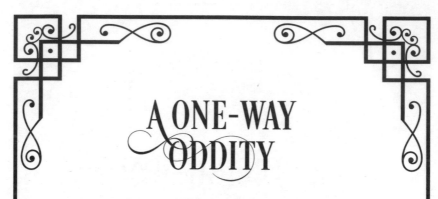

One afternoon, while I stayed in to type up some case notes, Holmes had a meeting with Lestrade.

"How did it go?" I asked him, when he returned.

"Oh, you know how it is," said Holmes dismissively. "He tells me his theories about a number of cases he's working on, and I explain to him why they are wrong."

"Of course," I said. "Nothing that might interest my readers, then?"

"Well, I suppose there was something that you might find worthy of note. As we were walking to his office from where we met, we passed a driver going the wrong way up a one-way street. And yet Lestrade did nothing about it."

"Did he not see the man?" I asked. "Or does he simply not consider traffic matters to be his domain?"

"Oh, he certainly saw the man," Holmes replied. "And I'm sure he would have intervened had he believed there had been reason to."

So why didn't Lestrade intervene?

The Reigate Squires continues from page 83

"Where I was sure it must be. I'll make the whole matter clear to you presently. I think, Colonel, that you and Watson might return now, and I will be with you again in an hour at the furthest. The inspector and I must have a word with the prisoners, but you will certainly see me back at luncheon time."

Sherlock Holmes was as good as his word, for about one o'clock he rejoined us in the colonel's smoking-room. He was accompanied by a little elderly gentleman, who was introduced to me as the Mr Acton whose house had been the scene of the original burglary.

"I wished Mr Acton to be present while I demonstrated this small matter to you," said Holmes, "for it is natural that he should take a keen interest in the details. I am afraid, my dear Colonel, that you must regret the hour that you took in such a stormy petrel as I am."

"On the contrary," answered the colonel, warmly, "I consider it the greatest privilege to have been permitted to study your methods of working. I confess that they quite surpass my expectations, and that I am utterly unable to account for your result. I have not yet seen the vestige of a clue."

"I am afraid that my explanation may disillusion you but it has always been my habit to hide none of my methods, either from my friend Watson or from anyone who might take an intelligent interest in them. But, first, as I am rather shaken by the knocking about which I had in the dressing-room, I think that I shall help myself to a dash of your brandy, Colonel. My strength has been rather tried of late."

"I trust that you had no more of those nervous attacks."

Sherlock Holmes laughed heartily. "We will come to that in its turn," said he. "I will lay an account of the case before you in its due order, showing you the various points which guided me in my decision. Pray interrupt me if there is any inference which is not perfectly clear to you.

"It is of the highest importance in the art of detection to be able to recognize, out of a number of facts, which are incidental and which vital. Otherwise your energy and attention must be dissipated instead of being concentrated. Now, in this case there was not the slightest doubt in my mind from the first that the key of the whole matter must be looked for in the scrap of paper in the dead man's hand.

"Before going into this, I would draw your attention to the fact that, if Alec Cunningham's narrative was correct, and if the assailant, after shooting William Kirwan, had instantly fled, then it obviously could not be he who tore the paper from the dead man's hand. But if it was not he, it must have been Alec Cunningham himself, for by the time that the old man had descended several servants were upon the scene. The point is a simple one, but the inspector had overlooked it because he had started with the supposition that these county magnates had had nothing to do with the matter. Now, I make a point of never having any prejudices, and of following docilely wherever fact may lead me, and so, in the very first stage of the investigation, I found myself looking a little askance at the part which had been played by Mr Alec Cunningham.

"And now I made a very careful examination of the corner of paper which the inspector had submitted to us. It was at once clear to me that it formed part of a very remarkable document. Here it is. Do you not now observe something very suggestive about it?"

"It has a very irregular look," said the colonel.

"My dear sir," cried Holmes, "there cannot be the least doubt in the world that it has been written by two persons doing alternate words. When I draw your attention to the strong t's of 'at' and 'to', and ask you to compare them with the weak ones of 'quarter' and 'twelve,' you will instantly recognize the fact. A very brief analysis of these four words would enable you to say with the utmost confidence that the 'learn' and the 'maybe' are written in the stronger hand, and the 'what' in the weaker."

"By Jove, it's as clear as day!" cried the colonel. "Why on earth should two men write a letter in such a fashion?"

"Obviously the business was a bad one, and one of the men who distrusted the other was determined that, whatever was done, each should have an equal hand in it. Now, of the two men, it is clear that the one who wrote the "at' and "to' was the ringleader."

"How do you get at that?"

the story continues on page 106

The Second Rebus

The Inspector was, as usual, having trouble with a case, and so had sent Holmes a list of suspects to interview, in the hope that he might be able to shed some light on the matter. However, when we arrived at the second house on the list, we found the following message pinned to the door, signed by Lestrade:

What did the message say?

THE SHIFTING BOX

Holmes and I were called to Scotland Yard to investigate the appearance of a mysterious box. The box was made of wood, and sealed. It had appeared on the floor of an interrogation room and one of the officers had, with only a small amount of exertion, lifted it onto the table. But since being placed on the table it seemed to have become several times heavier, and now no single officer was capable of lifting it up.

Holmes and I went into the room, where several police officers were guarding the box with suspicion. Holmes walked over to the box and gave the top a sharp knock, making everyone jump. He then tapped the metal table.

"Gentlemen, may I make a guess as to what is inside this box?"

What did he guess?

THE DOOR DILEMMA

I recently had the privilege of accompanying Holmes to Buckingham Palace, for an audience with Her Majesty (readers will be disappointed to learn that I am unable to disclose the purpose of our visit). We were met at the palace gates by two guards, one of whom greeted us warmly, shaking our hands in turn, and the other of whom remained sullen and silent, barely acknowledging our arrival. Holmes, evidently amused by this disparity and untroubled by the prospect of insulting the guards by commenting on it, turned to me with an amused expression on his face.

"I say, Watson, this gives me an idea for an excellent riddle."

I tried to wordlessly signal to him that I thought this was neither the time nor the place for riddle-posing, but as ever he was not to be deterred.

"Imagine that there are two doors to a palace: one that leads directly to the throne room and one that takes you straight down to the dungeons. Moreover, these doors are guarded by two guards: one who always tells the truth, and one who always lies. You are in urgent need of an audience with Her Majesty, but when you arrive at one of the doors you do not know whether the guard in front of it is the truth-teller or the liar. What question should you ask the guard to ensure that you are going through the right door?"

THE CAKE TRIOS

Mrs. Hudson is not perhaps a natural cook, but she has been known to dabble in the baking arts every now and then. On one occasion, she made nine small cakes, storing three each in three tins of different sizes, before later telling us to help ourselves. But before I could tuck in, Holmes interrupted.

"Wait a moment, Watson. Before you devour the cakes, no doubt tin and all, I have a proposition for you. If you can eat three cakes, yet leave each tin still with three cakes in it, then I will give up my share and let you have the remaining cakes."

How could I do it?

The Scone Problem

I was partaking of a cup of tea with both Holmes and Mrs. Hudson, when Mrs. Hudson produced a plate of scones: some plain, some containing raisins, and some containing chocolate chips. She passed them first to Holmes and he selected one containing raisins. Now, quite frankly I have never understood why raisin scones need to exist, and I believe that Holmes pretends to enjoy them purely because he knows the disdain I hold them in.

In any case, having made his own dubious choice, Holmes turned to me, saying, "Watson, a challenge! I am considering handing you a scone of my own choice. Now, if you can make a true statement about what I am about to do then I will give you that scone, but make a false one and I will give you nothing. Now, what true statement can you make to me that will guarantee yourself the scone of your choice?"

Given my preference for a chocolate chip scone, what statement should I have made?

WET CLOTHES

I foolishly made the mistake of heading out to the corner shop in mid-November without an umbrella, and naturally on my return it was raining most heavily. I made haste back to 221B but still I became thoroughly drenched. To compound my suffering, Mrs. Hudson was passing through the hallway just as I got back and was not impressed.

"Now, Mr. Watson," she said. "I've just cleaned the carpet and I won't have you dripping all over it."

"What would you have me do instead, Mrs. Hudson?" I asked, wringing my hands as I attempted to wring out my clothes.

"I'll put down some newspaper," she declared. "Just wait there, I won't be a moment."

While all this was going on Holmes overheard our conversation and came down to investigate.

"You're looking rather wet, old chap," he said helpfully.

I sighed. "Yes, I think my clothes were about 99 per cent water after going through that downpour," I told him. "And, having wrung them out for ten minutes on the doorstep, I think they're now about 98 per cent water."

"There's an interesting question in this," said Holmes. "Let us say that your clothes weighed 20 ounces when you first got here, with 99 per cent of that weight being water. If you've now wrung them out so that only 98 per cent of their weight is water, then how much do they weigh now?"

THE SLOW WORKMEN

Scotland Yard was being refurbished, and a large part of this seemed to involve painting. There were four different men working there, and they seemed to be present at every corner of the building, ready with precarious ladders and large buckets of paint just waiting to be crashed into and tipped over. Moreover, they appeared to be working at an unimaginably slow rate.

"Honestly," I said to Holmes, "I'm certain it's taken them four days to paint just the four walls of the reception room. I dread to think how long it will take for them to finish the building."

I saw from the look on his face that my frustrated comment would not be met in kind, but had engendered in his mind the kind of riddle that I frequently strove to avoid.

"Here's a question for you, then, Watson," Holmes responded. "If it takes four men four days to paint four walls, how many men would it take to paint one hundred walls in one hundred days?"

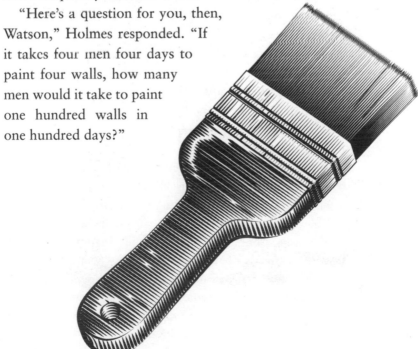

The Reigate Squires continues from page 95

"We might deduce it from the mere character of the one hand as compared with the other. But we have more assured reasons than that for supposing it. If you examine this scrap with attention you will come to the conclusion that the man with the stronger hand wrote all his words first, leaving blanks for the other to fill up. These blanks were not always sufficient, and you can see that the second man had a squeeze to fit his 'quarter' in between the 'at' and the 'to,' showing that the latter were already written. The man who wrote all his words first is undoubtedly the man who planned the affair."

"Excellent!" cried Mr Acton.

"But very superficial," said Holmes. "We come now, however, to a point which is of importance. You may not be aware that the deduction of a man's age from his writing is one which has been brought to considerable accuracy by experts. In normal cases one can place a man in his true decade with tolerable confidence. I say normal cases, because ill-health and physical weakness reproduce the signs of old age, even when the invalid is a youth. In this case, looking at the bold, strong hand of the one, and the rather broken-backed appearance of the other, which still retains its legibility although the t's have begun to lose their crossings, we can say that the one was a young man and the other was advanced in years without being positively decrepit."

"Excellent!" cried Mr Acton again.

"There is a further point, however, which is subtler and of greater interest. There is something in common between these hands. They belong to men who are blood-relatives. It may be most obvious to you in the Greek e's, but to me there are many small points which indicate the same thing. I have no doubt at all that a family mannerism can be traced in these two specimens of writing. I am only, of course, giving you the leading results now of my examination of the paper. There were twenty-three other deductions which would be of more interest to experts than to you. They all tend to deepen the impression upon my mind that the Cunninghams, father and son, had written this letter.

"Having got so far, my next step was, of course, to examine into the details of the crime, and to see how far they would help us. I went up to the house with the inspector, and saw all that was to be seen. The wound upon the dead man was, as I was able to determine with absolute confidence, fired from a revolver at the distance of something over four yards. There was no powder-blackening on the clothes. Evidently, therefore, Alec Cunningham had lied when he said that the two men were struggling when the shot was fired. Again, both father and son agreed as to the place where the man escaped into the road. At that point, however, as it happens, there is a broadish ditch, moist at the bottom. As there were no indications of bootmarks about this ditch, I was absolutely sure not only that the Cunninghams had again lied, but that there had never been any unknown man upon the scene at all.

"And now I have to consider the motive of this singular crime. To get at this, I endeavoured first of all to solve the reason of the original burglary at Mr Acton's. I understood, from something which the colonel told us, that a lawsuit had been going on between you, Mr Acton, and the Cunninghams. Of course, it instantly occurred to me that they had broken into your library with the intention of getting at some document which might be of importance in the case."

"Precisely so," said Mr Acton. "There can be no possible doubt as to their intentions. I have the clearest claim upon half of their present estate, and if they could have found a single paper—which, fortunately, was in the strongbox of my solicitors—they would undoubtedly have crippled our case."

"There you are," said Holmes, smiling. "It was a dangerous, reckless attempt, in which I seem to trace the influence of young Alec. Having found nothing they tried to divert suspicion by making it appear to be an ordinary burglary, to which end they carried off whatever they could lay their hands upon. That is all clear enough, but there was much that was still obscure. What I wanted above all was to get the missing part of that note. I was certain that Alec had torn it out of the dead man's hand, and almost certain that he must have thrust it into the pocket of his dressing-gown. Where else could he have put it?...

the story continues on page 118

A SECOND CODED MESSAGE

The second coded message Holmes and I received was a tip-off about an art heist we were investigating. We had so far managed to track down three of four stolen paintings, but the fourth as yet eluded us. That was, at least, until the following message was slipped under our door one day on a torn-off scrap of paper:

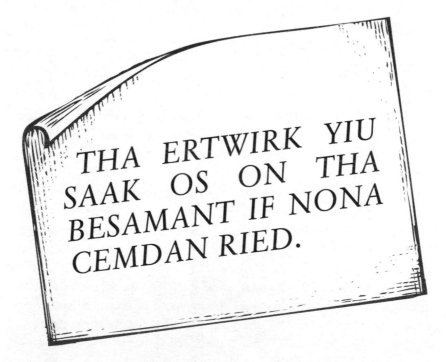

THA ERTWIRK YIU SAAK OS ON THA BESAMANT IF NONA CEMDAN RIED.

So where was the painting?

AN ODD ORDER

Holmes arrived home at our chambers late one evening, while I was busy reading a most fascinating report in the evening edition of the newspaper that I will perhaps tell you about some other time.

"Watson, there are two men standing outside our front door. A Scot and an Irishman, if I'm not mistaken."

I looked up from my paper with alarm. "Do you think they mean us harm?"

"No, no, I don't think they're here for us at all," he said, to my great relief and minor confusion. "I mention them because of the unusual way they are standing. You see, the Scot was standing behind the Irishman, and the Irishman was standing behind the Scot."

How was this curious arrangement possible?

The Fifth Deduction

Scotland Yard had a rather intriguing case for which Holmes and I were called in to consult. There had been a jewel heist and the police were now trying to intercept the jewels as they made their way from the crooks' storehouses to the river docks, before they were smuggled out of the country.

The police had identified four storehouses, one in the North of London, one in the East, one in the West, and one in the South. Moreover, they knew that the four storehouses were shipping their jewels on consecutive days, from Monday through to Thursday. In each storehouse was stashed a different kind of jewel: sapphires in one, emeralds in another, diamonds in the third, and rubies in the fourth. In addition, the four crooks involved in the heist, each of whom was taking care of one of the shipments, each had a different codename: Red, Green, Blue, or Yellow.

In order to have the best chance of recovering all of the stolen jewels, the police wanted our help in identifying which storehouse contained which type of jewel, when it was planned to ship them, and who was in charge of the shipment.

The officers had managed to retrieve the following set of clues:

The North storehouse will be shipping its product after the rubies have been shipped.

No crook's jewels are the same hue as their codename.

Green's shipment is the final one.

The West storehouse is shipping sapphires one day after Blue's shipment.

Yellow's shipment is on Tuesday.

The diamonds are being shipped from the East storehouse, before the emeralds and sapphires.

From this information, can you deduce all of the information that the police require?

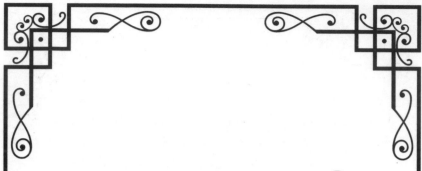

SLEEPING IT OFF

"My friend told me the strangest story the other day," said Mrs. Hudson, as we joined her for tea. "A cousin of hers was married to a man who was plagued with nightmares about being beheaded. One night, the man was having this same dream again, and just as the axe was being swung his wife tapped him on the back of the neck to wake him up and stop him snoring. Well, the shock of it gave the poor man a heart attack, and he died on the spot!"

"I'm afraid your friend was pulling your leg," said Holmes solemnly.

"Yes," I agreed. "It does sound a bit unlikely."

"Unlikely? I should say it was impossible for it to have happened as Mrs. Hudson reported it."

Why did Holmes think the story could not be true?

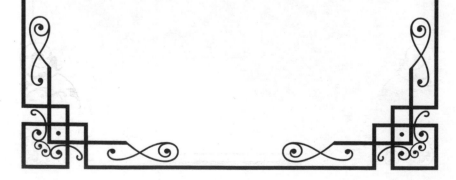

GETTING THE CHOP

Holmes and I were investigating a rather shady character who worked as a butcher. Holmes had popped into the shop for some reconnaissance and reported back to me when he returned to Baker Street.

"He's a tall man, Watson—over six feet, at a guess. Strong arms, and mean little eyes."

I noted these details down. "And what does he weigh, would you say, Holmes?"

At this, Holmes smiled. "Why, Watson, I should think that was obvious."

What did the man weigh?

The Case of the Secret Sailors

During one of our more fantastical cases, Holmes and I found ourselves investigating the goings-on of a secret society of sailors. After much careful inquiry and coordination with the Baker Street Irregulars, we managed to locate their headquarters. Once inside, we were met with a front desk. Above the desk were two crossed flags and, more curiously, above them was a row of seven clocks. My first thought was that these clocks might be recording the time in different parts of the world, but a quick glance at them made it clear that this was not the case. From left to right, the clock times were as follows: five past three, half past one, twenty to two, ten to seven, five to ten, twenty to four, and five past six.

At the desk was a tall, pallid man in a navy suit. He appeared to appraise us for a moment before saying: "Entry word, please."

Nonplussed, I looked at Holmes, who was of course able to respond immediately.

What was the appropriate password that he was requesting?

IRREGULAR TWINS

Having spent a fair amount of time with the Baker Street Irregulars, I remarked to Holmes that an unusual number of them were twins.

"Ah yes, well that can come in handy," he replied, "what with the possibility of trading places and so forth."

"Oh dear!" exclaimed Mrs. Hudson, who was sitting with us. "You've reminded me, Mr. Holmes. It was my great niece Jane's birthday yesterday, and I clean forgot all about it!" She stood up abruptly. "It's her twin Margaret's birthday tomorrow. I'd better try and get them both something in time for that."

"Holmes," I said, as Mrs. Hudson hurried off. "Do you think our dear landlady is quite alright? She seems to think that twins can have birthdays two days apart!"

"I have every confidence that Mrs. Hudson is perfectly sound of mind," Holmes reassured me.

But how could it be that one twin's birthday is two days after the other?

The Reigate Squires continues from page 107

...The only question was whether it was still there. It was worth an effort to find out, and for that object we all went up to the house.

"The Cunninghams joined us, as you doubtless remember, outside the kitchen door. It was, of course, of the very first importance that they should not be reminded of the existence of this paper, otherwise they would naturally destroy it without delay. The inspector was about to tell them the importance which we attached to it when, by the luckiest chance in the world, I tumbled down in a sort of fit and so changed the conversation.

"Good heavens!" cried the colonel, laughing, "do you mean to say all our sympathy was wasted and your fit an imposture?"

"Speaking professionally, it was admirably done," cried I, looking in amazement at this man who was forever confounding me with some new phase of his astuteness.

"It is an art which is often useful," said he. "When I recovered I managed, by a device which had perhaps some little merit of ingenuity, to get old Cunningham to write the word 'twelve', so that I might compare it with the 'twelve' upon the paper."

"Oh, what an ass I have been!" I exclaimed.

"I could see that you were commiserating with me over my weakness," said Holmes, laughing. "I was sorry to cause you the sympathetic pain which I know that you felt. We then went upstairs together, and having entered the room and seen the dressing-gown hanging up behind the door, I contrived, by upsetting a table, to engage their attention for the moment, and slipped back to examine the pockets. I had hardly got the paper, however—which was, as I had expected, in one of them—when the two Cunninghams were on me, and would, I verily believe, have murdered me then and there but for your prompt and friendly aid. As it is, I feel that young man's grip on my throat now, and the father has twisted my wrist round in the effort to get the paper out of my hand. They saw that I must know all about it, you see, and the sudden change from absolute security to complete despair made them perfectly desperate.

"I had a little talk with old Cunningham afterwards as to the motive of the crime. He was tractable enough, though his son was a perfect demon, ready to blow out his own or anybody else's brains if he could have got to his revolver. When Cunningham saw that the case against him was so strong he lost all heart and made a clean breast of everything. It seems that William had secretly followed his two masters on the night when they made their raid upon Mr Acton's, and having thus got them into his power, proceeded, under threats of exposure, to levy blackmail upon them. Mr Alec, however, was a dangerous man to play games of that sort with. It was a stroke of positive genius on his part to see in the burglary scare which was convulsing the countryside an opportunity of plausibly getting rid of the man whom he feared. William was decoyed up and shot, and had they only got the whole of the note and paid a little more attention to detail in the accessories, it is very possible that suspicion might never have been aroused."

"And the note?" I asked.

Sherlock Holmes placed the subjoined paper before us.

> If you will only come round at quarter to twelve to the east gate you will learn what will very much surprise you and maybe be of the greatest service to you and also to Annie Morrison. But say nothing to anyone upon the matter

"It is very much the sort of thing that I expected," said he. "Of course, we do not yet know what the relations may have been between Alec Cunningham, William Kirwan, and Annie Morrison. The result shows that the trap was skillfully baited. I am sure that you cannot fail to be delighted with the traces of heredity shown in the p's and in the tails of the g's. The absence of the i-dots in the old man's writing is also most characteristic. Watson, I think our quiet rest in the country has been a distinct success, and I shall certainly return much invigorated to Baker Street tomorrow."

THE END

A PUDDLE PUZZLE

Standing too close to the carriageway on my way home, I got badly splashed by a passing hackney. Arriving through the door, sopping wet and desperate for a change of clothes, I was met by Holmes. He was typically unsympathetic to my plight, and instead took the opportunity to spring a riddle on me.

"You've reminded me of one of the first riddles I ever heard, Watson. Pray, tell me: what is it that gets wetter as it dries?"

THE TERTIARY SEQUENCE

I had hoped, after the first two sequences Holmes sprang on me, that he would give up on the game, but clearly this was his current mental torment of choice. My wishes remaining unfulfilled, he hit me with a third sequence only a month later:

"Y, Y, H, L, Y, E, Y, T, R, R, R."

What comes next in this sequence?

THE STRANGE SHIPWRECK

"Watson," Holmes said, putting down his newspaper one morning, "have you read about the terrible nautical incident that happened yesterday?"

"I'm not sure I have," I replied. "What was it?"

"A boat sailing from America to England sank just off the coast of New York."

"Oh, that is terrible news!" I replied. "How many people were on board?"

"About a thousand people," he said. "But here's a puzzle: where will they bury the survivors?"

I considered this for a moment. "Their place of birth would be the most logical place, I suppose."

"Are you quite sure about that?" Holmes asked, with an arched eyebrow.

What would you suggest?

A PALINDROMIC PUZZLE

Curious as to my writing output, one slow weekend I decided to count how many words I had written in a report of a previous case. After many hours counting, during which I rewarded myself with many generous breaks, I finally reached the grand total of 24,942 words. I jubilantly reported this number to Holmes.

"That's a nice palindromic number you have there, Watson," remarked that prodigious brain. "But now that you have at last finished counting, here's something further to consider: how many more words would you have to write in order to reach the next palindromic number?"

RACING RESULTS

Holmes and I were at the dog track, as research for a case that I will certainly report on in full at the soonest opportunity. While we were there, Holmes—in his usual way—could not resist posing me a teaser or two from the expansive, seemingly inexhaustible collection that sits within his brain.

Holmes posed me the following question:

"See how there are eight dogs on the track. Now tell me, Watson, as quick as you can, if a dog begins to outrun the others and overtakes the dog in second place, what place is that dog in now?"

I answered him that of course the dog was now in first place, that being one better than second, to which Holmes responded with nothing more than an arched eyebrow and the following additional teaser:

"If a dog has just overtaken the dog in last position, what position is that dog in now?"

This seemed so obvious that I barely needed to tell him that the dog was now clearly one from last, or in Holmes' specific example with eight dogs it must now be in seventh position.

"Ah, Watson. You have made two false conclusions."

And so I had. What were they?

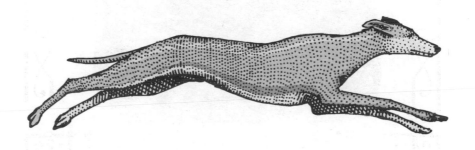

CARNIVAL CAKES

Holmes and I once found ourselves, during one of our investigations, at a village fair. It had a number of amusing games and activities for visitors to participate in, one of which was that most bizarre of sports: guessing the weight of a cake. There was a young couple in front of us, of which the gentleman put in a guess of 57 ounces, while the young lady followed up with a guess of 61 ounces. Holmes went next, and suggested that the cake weighed the more generous sum of 76 ounces. But I, feeling he was likely to be close but may have overestimated a little, put in a guess of 74 ounces.

The fellow running the stall later informed us of the correct weight of the cake, and it transpired that one of us had been 2 ounces out, one of us 4 ounces out, one of us 11 out and the other 15 out. Given this, whose guess had been the closest?

MATCHING SOCKS

Early one winter morning Holmes and I were summoned out of the city for an urgent case. Holmes tasked me with packing us both three nights' worth of clothes for the trip, but, out of a desire not to alert the rest of the street to our departure, he refused to turn on the light to enable me to see what I was doing.

Sleep-fuddled and irritated, I called to him angrily from my bedroom.

"You may not care about how you look, Holmes, but I want to give the impression of respectability. That is clearly impossible to do when I can't even see the clothes I'm packing. I've got both white and yellow socks in this drawer, with ten pairs of each. I'm going to have to pack darn near the whole lot to ensure I've got enough matching pairs."

"Nonsense," came the cheery reply from the next room. "Just apply a little mental acuity, my dear Watson, and you'll soon discover you need do nothing of the sort."

How many socks did I need to take from the drawer to ensure that I had three matching pairs?

HOLMES, SCRAMBLED

Tired of the constant challenges Holmes was setting me, I decided to set him one of my own.

"Here's a conundrum for you, Holmes. How long a word you can make from your own full name? That is, to say, from the letters SHERLOCKHOLMES?"

"Well, Watson," Holmes replied, "that quite depends. Am I allowed to re-use letters more than the number of times they appear in my name or not?"

I thought about this for a moment. "Well, how about you give me both answers. Both with re-using letters, and without."

After some thought, he responded: "Alright, then. I should say the longest word allowing re-use of the letters is some twelve letters long, although there are a good many more with eleven, and the longest word without re-using letters is nine letters long."

He was, as far as I could ascertain, quite right of course. Can you identify the words Holmes had in mind? Or find words that are almost as long?

THE MUSGRAVE RITUAL

An original short story by Sir Arthur Conan Doyle

An anomaly which often struck me in the character of my friend Sherlock Holmes was that, although in his methods of thought he was the neatest and most methodical of mankind, and although also he affected a certain quiet primness of dress, he was none the less in his personal habits one of the most untidy men that ever drove a fellow-lodger to distraction. Not that I am in the least conventional in that respect myself. The rough-and-tumble work in Afghanistan, coming on the top of a natural Bohemianism of disposition, has made me rather more lax than befits a medical man. But with me there is a limit, and when I find a man who keeps his cigars in the coal-scuttle, his tobacco in the toe end of a Persian slipper, and his unanswered correspondence transfixed by a jack-knife into the very centre of his wooden mantelpiece, then I begin to give myself virtuous airs. I have always held, too, that pistol practice should be distinctly an open-air pastime; and when Holmes, in one of his queer humours, would sit in an arm-chair with his hair-trigger and a hundred Boxer cartridges, and proceed to adorn the opposite wall with a patriotic V. R. done in bullet-pocks, I felt strongly that neither the atmosphere nor the appearance of our room was improved by it.

Our chambers were always full of chemicals and of criminal relics which had a way of wandering into unlikely positions, and of turning up in the butter-dish or in even less desirable places. But his papers were my great crux. He had a horror of destroying documents, especially those which were connected with his past cases, and yet it was only once in every year or two that he would muster energy to docket and arrange them; for, as I have mentioned somewhere in these incoherent memoirs, the outbursts of passionate energy when he performed the remarkable feats with which his name is associated were followed by reactions of lethargy during which he would lie about with his violin and his books, hardly moving save from the sofa to the table. Thus month after month his papers accumulated, until every corner of the room was stacked with bundles of manuscript which were on no account to be burned, and which could not be put away save by their owner. One winter's night, as we sat together by the fire, I ventured to suggest to him that, as he had finished pasting extracts into his commonplace book, he might employ the next two hours in making our room a little more habitable. He could not deny the justice of my request, so with a rather rueful face he went off to his bedroom, from which he returned presently pulling a large tin box behind him. This he placed in the middle of the floor and, squatting down upon a stool in front of it, he threw back the lid. I could see that it was already a third full of bundles of paper tied up with red tape into separate packages.

"There are cases enough here, Watson," said he, looking at me with mischievous eyes. "I think that if you knew all that I had in this box you would ask me to pull some out instead of putting others in."

"These are the records of your early work, then?" I asked. "I have often wished that I had notes of those cases."

"Yes, my boy, these were all done prematurely before my biographer had come to glorify me." He lifted bundle after bundle in a tender, caressing sort of way. "They are not all successes, Watson," said he. "But there are some pretty little problems among them. Here's the record of the Tarleton murders, and the case of Vamberry, the wine merchant, and the adventure of the old Russian woman, and the singular affair of the aluminium crutch, as well as a full account of Ricoletti of the club-foot, and his abominable wife. And here—ah, now, this really is something a little recherché."

He dived his arm down to the bottom of the chest, and brought up a small wooden box with a sliding lid, such as children's toys are kept in. From within he produced a crumpled piece of paper, an old-fashioned brass key, a peg of wood with a ball of string attached to it, and three rusty old discs of metal.

"Well, my boy, what do you make of this lot?" he asked, smiling at my expression.

"It is a curious collection."

"Very curious, and the story that hangs round it will strike you as being more curious still."

"These relics have a history then?"

"So much so that they are history."

the story continues on page 142

COMMON PROPERTY TWO

I found another of Holmes' written collections of words while clearing out a cupboard one day. This time, the words were as follows:

Advocate

Attribute

Contract

Entrance

Project

Refuse

I wondered why he had kept this list, but then I eventually spotted the connection. Can you identify their common property?

AN ILLUMINATING PROBLEM

Holmes and I were investigating a suspected haunting—which turned out, of course, to be nothing of the sort—in a run-down mansion on the edge of the city. There were four switches in the reception room, one of which was for that room's light, but the other three were for rooms which were not visible from the reception room itself. While Holmes was examining the reception room, he tasked me with figuring out which of the switches was for the cellar, where the supposed apparition had been sighted.

"Surely it would be more efficient for you to help me?" I complained, not keen to make the steep descent into the cellar any more times than was necessary.

"Nonsense!" Holmes said. "If you put your mind to it you'll soon see that you need only make one trip."

What method did Holmes have in mind?

A STRANGELY SHAPED RIDDLE

Sometimes Holmes will spring a riddle on me before I even have both my feet through the door:

"Watson," he said, the moment he saw my face, "can you think of an item which comes in a variety of sizes, materials, and shapes, and is straight in some parts and rounded in others? It can be put wherever you may care to put it, and is often lost or misplaced, but there is only one place it truly belongs."

What item did Holmes have in mind?

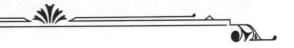

TRUTH-TELLERS AND LIARS

Holmes values nothing more than the power of pure deductive reasoning, so he is a dedicated enthusiast of that particular breed of logic puzzle involving those who always tell the truth and those who always lie. One I particularly enjoy involves a man visiting an island populated by only such people—let us call them "Truth-tellers" and "Liars"—who sees a beautiful woman there who he asks to take to dinner.

The woman replies, "I will go to dinner with you if and only if I am a Truth-teller."

So should the man make a reservation?

The Poisoned Party

We investigated a rather unpleasant affair last summer, which involved a number of deaths at a retired colonel's seventieth birthday party. The cause of death was determined to be poison, and Holmes and I did our best to find out from the surviving partygoers whether there was anything that had been consumed in common by all the victims, and no one else, so we could ascertain how the poison had been administered. But out of all the food, there was no item that had not been consumed by both victim and survivor alike, and as for drinks, we established that not all of the victims had drunk the champagne. That left the iced punch, which had, it seemed, been drunk by all the victims, but the Colonel himself had also drunk some and survived.

"And just how much of the punch did you drink?" Holmes asked him.

"Oh, I had a reasonably big glass at the beginning," the Colonel replied. "But after that I didn't have much time for eating or drinking, as I was busy entertaining my guests."

Holmes nodded. "Just as I thought." He turned to me. "Well, Watson, I think we've found the source of the poison."

What was it?

A Third Coded Message

The third coded message Holmes and I received pointed us towards a potential source of information about a murderer, which indeed later turned out to be instrumental.

We had narrowed down our list of suspects to just a few men, when the following message arrived:

What was the intention of this message?

The Musgrave Ritual continues from page 131

"What do you mean by that?"

Sherlock Holmes picked them up one by one, and laid them along the edge of the table. Then he reseated himself in his chair and looked them over with a gleam of satisfaction in his eyes.

"These," said he, "are all that I have left to remind me of the adventure of the Musgrave Ritual."

I had heard him mention the case more than once, though I had never been able to gather the details. "I should be so glad," said I, "if you would give me an account of it."

"And leave the litter as it is?" he cried, mischievously. "Your tidiness won't bear much strain after all, Watson. But I should be glad that you should add this case to your annals, for there are points in it which make it quite unique in the criminal records of this or, I believe, of any other country. A collection of my trifling achievements would certainly be incomplete which contained no account of this very singular business.

"You may remember how the affair of the *Gloria Scott*, and my conversation with the unhappy man whose fate I told you of, first turned my attention in the direction of the profession which has become my life's work. You see me now when my name has become known far and wide, and when I am generally recognized both by the public and by the official force as being a final court of appeal in doubtful cases. Even when you knew me first, at the time of the affair which you have commemorated in A *Study in Scarlet*, I had already established a considerable, though not a very lucrative, connection. You can hardly realize, then, how difficult I found it at first, and how long I had to wait before I succeeded in making any headway.

"When I first came up to London I had rooms in Montague Street, just round the corner from the British Museum, and there I waited, filling in my too abundant leisure time by studying all those branches of science which might make me more efficient. Now and again cases came in my way, principally through the introduction of old fellow-students, for during my last years at the university there was a good deal of talk there about myself and my methods. The third of these cases was that of the Musgrave Ritual, and it is to the interest which was aroused by that singular chain of events, and the large issues which proved to be at stake, that I trace my first stride towards the position which I now hold.

"Reginald Musgrave had been in the same college as myself, and I had some slight acquaintance with him. He was not generally popular among the undergraduates, though it always seemed to me that what was set down as pride was really an attempt to cover extreme natural diffidence. In appearance he was a man of exceedingly aristocratic type, thin, high-nosed, and large-eyed, with languid and yet courtly manners. He was indeed a scion of one of the very oldest families in the kingdom, though his branch was a cadet one which had separated from the northern Musgraves some time in the sixteenth century, and had established itself in western Sussex, where the Manor House of Hurlstone is perhaps the oldest inhabited building in the county. Something of his birthplace seemed to cling to the man, and I never looked at his pale, keen face or the poise of his head without associating him with grey archways and mullioned windows and all the venerable wreckage of a feudal keep. Once or twice we drifted into talk, and I can remember that more than once he expressed a keen interest in my methods of observation and inference.

"For four years I had seen nothing of him until one morning he walked into my room in Montague Street. He had changed little, was dressed like a young man of fashion—he was always a bit of a dandy—and preserved the same quiet, suave manner which had formerly distinguished him.

"'How has all gone with you Musgrave?' I asked, after we had cordially shaken hands.

"'You probably heard of my poor father's death,' said he; 'he was carried off about two years ago. Since then I have of course had the Hurlstone estates to manage, and as I am member for my district as well, my life has been a busy one. But I understand, Holmes, that you are turning to practical ends those powers with which you used to amaze us?'

the story continues on page 154

SUMMATION SORCERY

Holmes and I once caught a con man posing as a magician, who at least had quite a knack for making people's money disappear.

"I have always been fascinated by the work of magicians," Holmes confessed, once we'd handed over our suspect to Inspector Lestrade. "What they do when they construct their tricks is much like a reverse-engineering of the work we do, Watson. While we show how the apparently impossible is possible, they make the possible seem impossible."

"Perhaps you should turn your hand to magic," I suggested. "Detective by day, magician by night. I can picture you quite clearly with a black cape and a magic wand, pulling a rabbit out of a hat."

"I certainly see the attraction," Holmes said, apparently unaware of my teasing. "In fact, I have collected a mental inventory of tricks over the years. But nothing too elaborate," he added. He reached into his coat pocket, rummaged around, and pulled out three dice. "Here's one, for example. Without me looking, I want you to roll these three dice and add up the total, but don't tell me the result."

I rolled them, getting a three, a two and a five, for a total of ten.

"Once you have done that, pick one of the three and find the number on the bottom of the dice, and add that to your total."

I picked up the two, revealing a five at the bottom, and added that, giving me a total of fifteen.

"Now, re-roll that same die, and add the new number to your total."

I re-rolled and this time I got a one, for a total of sixteen.

"Now," Holmes said, turning around. "Remember that I do not know which of these dice you re-rolled, nor what number it showed to begin with." He looked briefly at the three numbers now shown by the dice. "Your total, if I am not mistaken, is sixteen."

How did he know?

The Island in the Lake

A mysterious disappearance once took Holmes to a house situated on a tiny island in the middle of a lake in the far north of England. When he got back, he told me of a curiosity he had encountered that he thought I might enjoy.

"On this island, Watson, there was a tractor. The strange thing was, there was not, and never had been, a bridge connecting the island to the mainland, and some investigation revealed to me that the tractor wasn't taken over by boat or air either, and neither was it assembled on the island. So it was quite the puzzle to me to establish how the tractor had arrived at its current location. Eventually, of course, I did hit upon the answer."

How did the tractor get onto the island?

USE YOUR HEAD

I came home from a weekend's stay with a friend in the countryside most disgruntled at the discovery that her fourteen-year-old son was now taller than I am.

"A full head taller than me!" I declaimed to Holmes. "It's an embarrassment! I shall have to start wearing shoes with thicker soles to compensate."

Holmes replied, "Well, Watson, I think you're wrong to put stock in such things. But here, let us take your mind off it a little. You have put me in a mind of a riddle."

He then asked me, "What is taller without a head than it is when it has a head on?"

What is the answer?

A FOURTH CODED MESSAGE

The fourth coded message we received came during one of our grizzliest cases: the brutal murder of Christopher Burns. At the time, we had only one suspect: Roger Cardwell, who was a student of Burns and thought to be a little disturbed. After a meeting between the two of them, Burns' body was found in a crumpled heap on the floor, limbs broken, neck bruised and eyes bloodshot.

Despite Holmes' intuitions to the contrary, the police were ready to take Cardwell in, until we received the following message:

RREGOS BEHTORR
SELGNARTD POSSEFORR
BNRUS

Upon decoding this, our investigation was given a new lease of life, and we were eventually able to catch the true culprit.

What did the message say?

The Lesser of Three Evils

"You are a criminal who has been tried and convicted," said Holmes.

"I don't remember that happening," I replied.

"When it comes to the sentencing," Holmes continued, "you are given a choice between three punishments. First, you may be hanged. Second, you may face the firing squad. Or third, you may be locked in a room with lions who haven't been fed for five weeks. Which do you choose?"

Which option would give me the highest chance of survival?

The Domino Deceit

I have always considered myself to be better with children than my famous colleague, but occasionally his powers of deduction can offer entertainment which goes down very well with a younger audience. One of the tricks I most enjoyed myself involved a set of dominoes which some children were amusing themselves with at the house of a client.

"Are you any good at dominoes, Mr. Holmes, sir?" asked one of the children as we passed through the drawing room.

"I have never had much use for the game itself," he replied, "but I do know a couple of tricks associated with it."

Naturally, the children pressed him to show them.

"Alright," he said at last. "Your task is to join the dominoes—like number to like number—so that they form one long line. I will then be able to tell you, without looking at your line, the numbers at either end of it."

He turned his back, and the children got to work joining the pieces.

"We're ready, Mr. Holmes," they proclaimed, mere moments later.

"Your numbers," Holmes declared, "are four and six."

The children erupted in squeals of amazement. But how did he know?

A LIKELY STORY

Mrs. Hudson's mischievous great nephew was once again in Baker Street, but on this visit he graduated to larceny, misappropriating a rather important note from Mrs. Hudson's purse. When we questioned him about it, he professed innocence, saying: "I didn't steal it, sirs. No, I found it in that book over there. She must have used it as a bookmark, and I remember for certain that I found it between pages 47 and 48, poking out the top of the book."

Holmes immediately knew he was lying. How?

The Musgrave Ritual continues from page 143

"'Yes,' said I, 'I have taken to living by my wits.'

"'I am delighted to hear it, for your advice at present would be exceedingly valuable to me. We have had some very strange doings at Hurlstone, and the police have been able to throw no light upon the matter. It is really the most extraordinary and inexplicable business.'

"You can imagine with what eagerness I listened to him, Watson, for the very chance for which I had been panting during all those months of inaction seemed to have come within my reach. In my inmost heart I believed that I could succeed where others failed, and now I had the opportunity to test myself.

"'Pray, let me have the details,' I cried.

"Reginald Musgrave sat down opposite to me, and lit the cigarette which I had pushed towards him.

"'You must know,' said he, 'that though I am a bachelor, I have to keep up a considerable staff of servants at Hurlstone, for it is a rambling old place, and takes a good deal of looking after. I preserve, too, and in the pheasant months I usually have a house-party, so that it would not do to be short-handed. Altogether there are eight maids, the cook, the butler, two footmen, and a boy. The garden and the stables of course have a separate staff.

"'Of these servants the one who had been longest in our service was Brunton the butler. He was a young schoolmaster out of place when he was first taken up by my father, but he was a man of great energy and character, and he soon became quite invaluable in the household. He was a well-grown, handsome man, with a splendid forehead, and though he has been with us for twenty years he cannot be more than forty now. With his personal advantages and his extraordinary gifts—for he can speak several languages and play nearly every musical instrument—it is wonderful that he should have been satisfied so long in such a position, but I suppose that he was comfortable, and lacked energy to make any change. The butler of Hurlstone is always a thing that is remembered by all who visit us.

"'But this paragon has one fault. He is a bit of a Don Juan, and you can imagine that for a man like him it is not a very difficult part to play in a quiet country district. When he was married it was all right, but since he has been a widower we have had no end of trouble with him. A few months ago we were in hopes that he was about to settle down again for he became engaged to Rachel Howells, our second housemaid; but he has thrown her over since then and taken up with Janet Tregellis, the daughter of the head gamekeeper. Rachel—who is a very good girl, but of an excitable Welsh temperament—had a sharp touch of brain-fever, and goes about the house now—or did until yesterday—like a black-eyed shadow of her former self. That was our first drama at Hurlstone; but a second one came to drive it from our minds, and it was prefaced by the disgrace and dismissal of butler Brunton.

"'This was how it came about. I have said that the man was intelligent, and this very intelligence has caused his ruin, for it seems to have led to an insatiable curiosity about things which did not in the least concern him. I had no idea of the lengths to which this would carry him, until the merest accident opened my eyes to it.

"'I have said that the house is a rambling one. One day last week—on Thursday night, to be more exact—I found that I could not sleep, having foolishly taken a cup of strong café noir after my dinner. After struggling against it until two in the morning, I felt that it was quite hopeless, so I rose and lit the candle with the intention of continuing a novel which I was reading. The book, however, had been left in the billiard-room, so I pulled on my dressing-gown and started off to get it.

"'In order to reach the billiard-room I had to descend a flight of stairs and then to cross the head of a passage which led to the library and the gunroom. You can imagine my surprise when, as I looked down this corridor, I saw a glimmer of light coming from the open door of the library. I had myself extinguished the lamp and closed the door before coming to bed. Naturally my first thought was of burglars. The corridors at Hurlstone have their walls largely decorated with trophies of old weapons. From one of these I picked a battle-axe, and then, leaving my candle behind me, I crept on tiptoe down the passage and peeped in at the open door.

the story continues on page 166

THE PARTY PROBLEM

Holmes and I, much to his dissatisfaction, had been compelled to attend a party for the deputy inspector's retirement. Holmes, therefore, felt the need to amuse himself by imposing problems on the assembled dignitaries. One that I particularly enjoyed concerned a large cake that sat portentously on a dais, waiting to be eaten at the conclusion of the evening's festivities.

"Watson, observe that cake. You will note that it is a perfect cylinder of consistent radius from bottom to top, and note also how completely smooth its top surface is. The baker is certainly an artisan. But it also reminds me of a rather satisfying puzzle, that I am sure you will have no trouble demolishing, as you will no doubt later also help demolish the cake itself."

I ignored Holmes' rather unkind reference to my liking for bakery products, and shortly afterwards he continued thus:

"Notice how there are eight people attending this event. Now, say that all eight of those people wish to have an exactly equal amount of cake, how would you best go about this?"

This seemed a not particularly complex challenge, until he also added:

"You may only use three cuts, and all eight pieces must be of the same shape and size."

What solution did he have in mind?

BRIDGE, INTERRUPTED

Holmes and I were invited to a game of bridge at a client's house. Part of the way through a round, the dealer was briefly summoned to another room, and when he returned none of us could remember how far around the table he had got with his dealing. For those uninitiated in the ways of bridge, the dealer must deal 13 cards each to four players, dealing clockwise from a pack of 52 cards.

Can you work out what Holmes' suggestion was for how to rectify the situation? Of course, social decorum had to be maintained and no dealt cards could be touched before the deal was complete, so we could not count how many had already been placed on the table.

ATOP THE
SHIPPING CONTAINER

On one particular case, Holmes was determined to examine the top of a large shipping container. The container was far too high for either of us to reach the top on our own, so Holmes suggested that he stand on my shoulders and try to grab the edge of the container and lift himself up.

Not fancying the idea of having Holmes on my shoulders, I objected. "Surely I should stand on your shoulders, Holmes? Lifting oneself up like that is no mean feat, and I think that sort of thing is more my area of expertise, if you don't mind my saying so."

"The physical challenge, of which I assure you I am quite capable, is not the issue, Watson. Even with one of us on the other's shoulders I'm not sure we'll reach the top, but as I am the taller of the two of us we have a better chance if I am on your shoulders."

Why was Holmes correct?

NEWSPAPER PAGES

"Watson," Holmes said to me over breakfast one morning, "how many pages does that newspaper of yours contain?"

I turned to the final page. "36," I told him.

"Nine sheets folded in half then, I imagine. So tell me Watson, if the first sheet of that newspaper contains pages 1, 2, 35 and 36, which pages share a sheet with page 28?"

TRUTH-TELLERS
AND LIARS
TWO

I ask you, dear reader, to recall our previous Truth-tellers and Liars case, in which a man visited the island of Truth-tellers and Liars and asked a woman to dinner. I will, however, remind you that all the people on this island tell only the truth, or tell only lies. Having professed to Holmes my enjoyment of that case, he presented me with a follow-up conundrum which resumed with the same characters.

The man and woman are still on their dinner date, and the woman does not know that the man is not a native of the island. Over the course of their conversation, it transpires that she only wants to date rich Liars.

What can the man say to convince her that he is a rich Liar, given that she assumes him to be either a) a rich Liar, b) a poor Liar, c) a rich Truth-teller, or d) a poor Truth-teller?

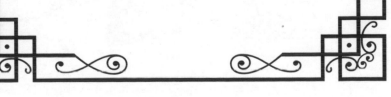

A FAIR RACE

Holmes and I were walking through Regent's Park when we saw two young boys limbering up for a race. Amused, we sat on a nearby bench to watch the spectacle. On a count of three they were off, and in not more than about ten seconds of wild running the taller of the two had reached his destination.

"Not exactly neck and neck, was it, Holmes?" I remarked. "I'd say that chap won by a good five yards. Perhaps they'd better apply some sort of handicap next time."

Holmes looked thoughtful. "I'd say they were running about 50 yards in total. So let's say we agree with your estimate that the taller boy won by five yards and, as such, we get him to start the race five yards behind the other. Do you think this measure would even things out?"

I pondered this scenario for a moment. Who would win, assuming they both ran at the same speeds again?

" 'Brunton, the butler, was in the library. He was sitting, fully dressed, in an easy-chair, with a slip of paper which looked like a map upon his knee, and his forehead sunk forward upon his hand in deep thought. I stood dumb with astonishment, watching him from the darkness. A small taper on the edge of the table shed a feeble light which sufficed to show me that he was fully dressed. Suddenly, as I looked, he rose from his chair, and walking over to a bureau at the side, he unlocked it and drew out one of the drawers. From this he took a paper, and returning to his seat he flattened it out beside the taper on the edge of the table, and began to study it with minute attention. My indignation at this calm examination of our family documents overcame me so far that I took a step forward, and Brunton, looking up, saw me standing in the doorway. He sprang to his feet, his face turned livid with fear, and he thrust into his breast the chart-like paper which he had been originally studying.

" ' "So!" said I. "This is how you repay the trust which we have reposed in you. You will leave my service tomorrow."

" 'He bowed with the look of a man who is utterly crushed, and slunk past me without a word. The taper was still on the table, and by its light I glanced to see what the paper was which Brunton had taken from the bureau. To my surprise it was nothing of any importance at all, but simply a copy of the questions and answers in the singular old observance called the Musgrave Ritual. It is a sort of ceremony peculiar to our family, which each Musgrave for centuries past has gone through on his coming of age—a thing of private interest, and perhaps of some little importance to the archaeologist, like our own blazonings and charges, but of no practical use whatever.'

" 'We had better come back to the paper afterwards,' said I.

" 'If you think it really necessary,' he answered, with some hesitation. 'To continue my statement, however: I relocked the bureau, using the key which Brunton had left, and I had turned to go when I was surprised to find that the butler had returned, and was standing before me.

" ' "Mr Musgrave, sir," he cried, in a voice which was hoarse with emotion, "I can't bear disgrace, sir. I've always been proud above my station in life, and disgrace would kill me. My blood will be on your head, sir—it will, indeed—if you drive me to despair. If you cannot keep me after what has passed, then for God's sake let me give you notice and leave in a month, as if of my own free will. I could stand that, Mr Musgrave, but not to be cast out before all the folk that I know so well."

" ' "You don't deserve much consideration, Brunton," I answered. "Your conduct has been most infamous. However, as you have been a long time in the family, I have no wish to bring public disgrace upon you. A month, however is too long. Take yourself away in a week, and give what reason you like for going."

" ' "Only a week, sir?" he cried, in a despairing voice. "A fortnight— say at least a fortnight!"

" ' "A week," I repeated, "and you may consider yourself to have been very leniently dealt with."

" 'He crept away, his face sunk upon his breast, like a broken man, while I put out the light and returned to my room.

" ' For two days after this Brunton was most assiduous in his attention to his duties. I made no allusion to what had passed, and waited with some curiosity to see how he would cover his disgrace. On the third morning, however he did not appear, as was his custom, after breakfast to receive my instructions for the day. As I left the dining-room I happened to meet Rachel Howells, the maid. I have told you that she had only recently recovered from an illness, and was looking so wretchedly pale and wan that I remonstrated with her for being at work.

" ' "You should be in bed," I said. "Come back to your duties when you are stronger."

" 'She looked at me with so strange an expression that I began to suspect that her brain was affected.

" ' "I am strong enough, Mr Musgrave," said she.

the story continues on page 178

A BANANA BARGAIN

"My gosh! There are some remarkable deals at the fruit market today!" Mrs. Hudson remarked to us on an otherwise unremarkable Tuesday morning. "There's 10 apples and 5 bananas for only 35 pence, saving a total of 5 pence; and there's 30 apples for only 50 pence, saving 10 pence; oh, and, best of all, I found 10 bananas and 10 oranges for only 100 pence. That last deal alone saves you an entire 20 pence."

"Well, Watson," said Holmes, as Mrs. Hudson took the fruits of her fruit-buying into the kitchen. "Based on the information Mrs. Hudson has just given us, could you tell me how much it would ordinarily cost to buy one apple, one banana, and one orange?"

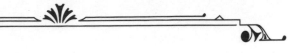

TARGET PRACTICE

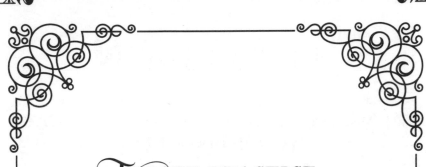

As has been known to happen on occasion, I came home to find Holmes engaged in revolver practice. A volley of shots went off as I approached the door, so I made certain to knock very loudly before entering.

"Yes, come in Watson!" Holmes called, and then immediately resumed shooting at a target he'd set up on the wall. "I'm getting some shooting practice in."

"Yes, I can see that."

"I'm trying to get my shots down to one every ten seconds," he explained. "But this past minute I only managed six."

"Well then you've done it, haven't you?" I asked.

"I have not, Watson, although I have made some significant progress."

How could Holmes be correct that he'd shot six bullets in sixty seconds and yet had not managed one bullet every ten seconds?

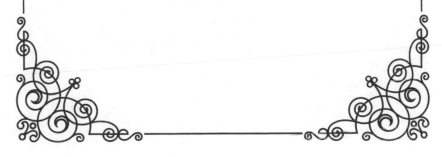

THE BROKEN FIVE

While investigating a case involving a mysterious theft, Holmes and I found ourselves in a printer's typesetting room. There appeared to have been some kind of a struggle, given the state of the furniture in the room, and as I looked around I noticed that thousands of numbers lay strewn across the floor. Most prominent of all was a large number "5", languishing in the middle of the floor.

"Looks like they'll have trouble typesetting any page numbers in the immediate future!" I remarked.

"Perhaps so," agreed Holmes. "In fact, Watson, that raises an interesting question. If you were to write every number from 1 to, let's say, 300, how many times would you write the digit 5?"

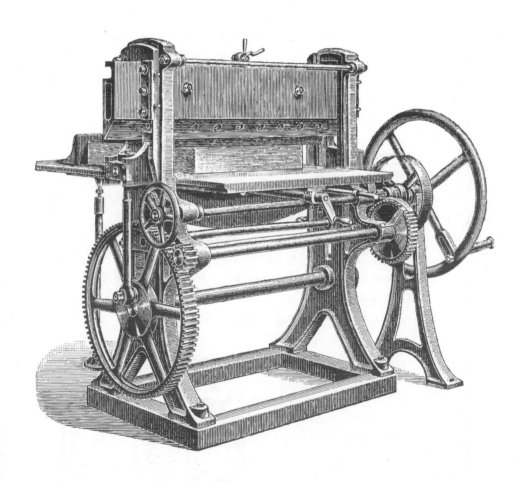

THE TRICKY TESTIMONY

Scotland Yard were investigating a mugging that had taken place in Regent's Park. The victim—a Mr. White—had reported being attacked by a man wearing blue dungarees with paint on the front and a brown cap pulled low over his eyes. The attacker had taken some very valuable items from Mr. White, so a full-scale investigation was launched. A number of people who were known or seen to have been in the park were questioned. One witness reported seeing a man who matched this exact description—cap, dungarees, paint stain—running out of the park toward Baker Street. Unfortunately, as the witness was behind the man, he obtained not even a glimpse of the man's face.

When Holmes heard about this report he frowned.

"I presume you held this witness for further questioning?"

"No, we let him go," said Inspector Lestrade. "He had nothing further to tell us."

"Nothing further?" Holmes exclaimed. "I should say your witness had a lot more to say, considering he lied in his testimony and was quite possibly involved in the crime!"

Why did Holmes think this?

Tying the Knot

I had been telling Holmes about a visit I had once had from an American acquaintance, when he sprung a rather odd question on me:

"Watson," he asked, "do you suppose that it is legal in New York for a man to marry his widow's sister?"

"Legal? Well, yes," I replied, "but frowned upon, I should think."

At this Holmes chuckled. "Frowned upon, indeed! Oh, Watson, you do amuse me."

Why did Holmes find my answer so funny?

A Table Tennis Trick

After the successful closure of a case, Holmes and I had been compelled to attend a celebratory dinner at the house of the wealthy client (much to Holmes' annoyance, it might be added). After dinner, it was suggested that we try out their new table tennis set. Unfortunately, however, there was only one ball to be found, and a particularly vigorous shot from a certain detective's assistant sent it flying out of the window, where it fell into a hole in a large stone garden feature. This hole was far too narrow for any of us to reach in and pick up the ball, and was too deep and dark for us to see exactly where it had come to rest. And yet, using only resources readily available to us, Holmes was able to retrieve the ball undamaged. How did he do it? I should also note that he did not damage the stone feature in any way.

THE CUBE QUANDARY

"Watson," said Holmes, "I am picturing a cube with each face either completely red or completely blue."

"That sounds like a waste of your mental talents," I replied.

"You are quite right, Watson, but it's your mental talents that concern me at this precise moment."

"Well I do wish they would stop concerning you quite so much!" I responded, exasperatedly.

"The more of these puzzles we do, the less concerned I will be," he chided. "Now, listen. About this cube: I want you to tell me how many possible combinations of face arrangements it could possibly have. To clarify, if one combination can be rotated so that it matches another combination, we will consider those the same combination."

"I must say, Holmes, with all these puzzles you throw at me I sometimes think you look forward to seeing my face completely red."

"Now, now, Watson, don't look so blue. This isn't a difficult one."

How many possible combinations are there?

BACTERIAL GROWTH

One particularly bizarre case took Holmes and myself to a laboratory where some odd-looking cultures were being grown in Petri dishes.

"Watson," Holmes said to me, in a way that suggested he was about to demonstrate his superior intellect. "Imagine that a Petri dish contains bacteria which divide in two every minute. If I tell you that there was a single bacterium at 9 a.m. and now, two and a half hours later at 11.30 a.m., the dish is half full, then at what time will the dish be full?"

" " "We will see what the doctor says," I answered. "You must stop work now, and when you go downstairs just say that I wish to see Brunton."

" " "The butler is gone," said she.

" " "Gone! Gone where?"

" " "He is gone. No one has seen him. He is not in his room. Oh, yes, he is gone, he is gone!" She fell back against the wall with shriek after shriek of laughter, while I, horrified at this sudden hysterical attack, rushed to the bell to summon help. The girl was taken to her room, still screaming and sobbing, while I made enquiries about Brunton. There was no doubt about it that he had disappeared. His bed had not been slept in, he had been seen by no one since he had retired to his room the night before, and yet it was difficult to see how he could have left the house, as both windows and doors were found to be fastened in the morning. His clothes, his watch, and even his money were in his room, but the black suit which he usually wore was missing. His slippers, too, were gone, but his boots were left behind. Where then could butler Brunton have gone in the night, and what could have become of him now?

" 'Of course we searched the house from cellar to garret, but there was no trace of him. It is, as I have said, a labyrinth of an old house, especially the original wing, which is now practically uninhabited; but we ransacked every room and cellar without discovering the least sign of the missing man. It was incredible to me that he could have gone away leaving all his property behind him, and yet where could he be? I called in the local police, but without success. Rain had fallen on the night before and we examined the lawn and the paths all round the house, but in vain. Matters were in this state, when a new development quite drew our attention away from the original mystery.

" 'For two days Rachel Howells had been so ill, sometimes delirious, sometimes hysterical, that a nurse had been employed to sit up with her at night. On the third night after Brunton's disappearance, the nurse, finding her patient sleeping nicely, had dropped into a nap in the armchair, when she woke in the early morning to find the bed empty, the window open, and no signs of the invalid. I was instantly aroused, and, with the two footmen, started off at once in search of the missing girl. It was not difficult to tell the direction which she had taken, for, starting from under her window, we could follow her footmarks easily across the lawn to the edge of the mere, where they vanished close to the gravel path which leads out of the grounds. The lake there is eight feet deep, and you can imagine our feelings when we saw that the trail of the poor demented girl came to an end at the edge of it.

"'Of course, we had the drags at once, and set to work to recover the remains, but no trace of the body could we find. On the other hand, we brought to the surface an object of a most unexpected kind. It was a linen bag which contained within it a mass of old rusted and discoloured metal and several dull-coloured pieces of pebble or glass. This strange find was all that we could get from the mere, and, although we made every possible search and enquiry yesterday, we know nothing of the fate either of Rachel Howells or of Richard Brunton. The county police are at their wits' end, and I have come up to you as a last resource.'

"You can imagine, Watson, with what eagerness I listened to this extraordinary sequence of events, and endeavoured to piece them together, and to devise some common thread upon which they might all hang. The butler was gone. The maid was gone. The maid had loved the butler, but had afterwards had cause to hate him. She was of Welsh blood, fiery and passionate. She had been terribly excited immediately after his disappearance. She had flung into the lake a bag containing some curious contents. These were all factors which had to be taken into consideration, and yet none of them got quite to the heart of the matter. What was the starting-point of this chain of events? There lay the end of this tangled line.

"'I must see that paper, Musgrave,' said I, 'which this butler of yours thought it worth his while to consult, even at the risk of the loss of his place.'

"'It is rather an absurd business, this ritual of ours,' he answered. 'But it has at least the saving grace of antiquity to excuse it. I have a copy of the questions and answers here if you care to run your eye over them.'

the story continues on page 190

A Textile Teaser

"I was visiting the old bazaar with Mrs. H the other day," remarked Holmes, "and as I passed by a clothing stand I was struck with the inspiration for a riddle—and I do know how you enjoy being perplexed by such trivial things."

"How kind," I replied, tersely.

"Tell me, Watson: what is it that is bought by the yard and yet worn by the foot?"

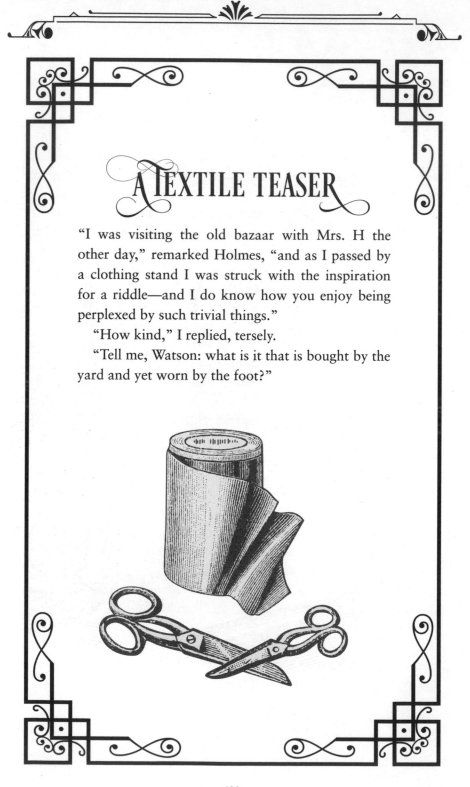

A FIFTH CODED MESSAGE

Holmes once told me that after the first twenty-four hours the probability of recovering a kidnap victim drops significantly. So when a girl named Adelia Atkins disappeared, we were under serious time pressure to find her, and could not afford to pursue all possible avenues. In terms of potential abductors, we considered her mother, Alexandra, and her father, Lucian, both of whom had been out of the city at the time of the disappearance. We also considered the nanny, Maria, who had been taking care of the girl and her brother James. And then there was the uncle, Charles, who had visited the children on the previous day.

Just before we set off from 221B to begin our investigation, we received the following note:

The note then appeared to have been torn, so that whatever followed was no longer attached.

"This is useless to us in this state, isn't it, Holmes?" I asked.

Holmes took the note and examined it for a moment. "On the contrary, Watson, it tells us exactly who we need to pursue."

Who was it?

A Psychic Paradox

Given Holmes' predilection for the pseudo-supernatural, we often find ourselves encountering those who fancy themselves to have a special connection to the occult.

"I simply cannot understand why these people must carry on as though they have magical abilities," I said, after yet another such episode. "It is as plain as day to anyone with a scientific mind that prediction of the future is impossible."

"I wouldn't be so hasty, Watson," Holmes replied. "Impossible is a strong word. Why, just the other day I saw it done."

How is it possible that Holmes saw someone predict the future?

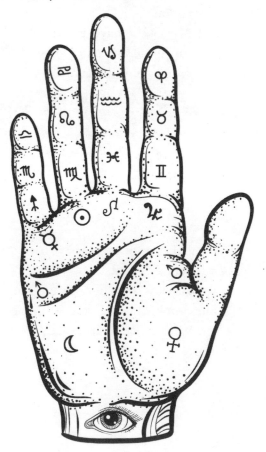

The Crossroads

Holmes and I were taking a carriage through an unfamiliar stretch of English countryside when we arrived at a crossroads. Moreover, some crude vandal had pushed over the marker indicating where each road led and discarded it in a nearby ditch, so we had no clue as to in which way our destination lay.

"What a bothersome thing to do!" I exclaimed, and our driver was quite in agreement.

"Now Watson, there's no need to get heated," said Holmes. "It's just a harmless prank."

"Harmless? We'll have to wait here for hours until someone comes along who can give us directions!"

"That would be quite unnecessary."

Holmes was right, of course. So how could we determine which way we ought to go?

THE THIRD REBUS

I rose early one Sunday morning, so I decided to make breakfast for Holmes, Mrs. Hudson, and myself. The kitchen cupboards contained eggs, bacon, and bread, but I thought I would ask the other two for their orders before I began cooking, so as not to cook more than was needed.

Mrs. Hudson kept things simple, requesting a piece of toast and a fried egg. Holmes, on the other hand, took the opportunity to be as cryptic as possible and, rather than saying anything, merely wrote down the following and then handed it to me:

What did Holmes want for breakfast?

A Close Shave

"Watson," Holmes said to me, "here's a little chin-scratcher for you. I interviewed a man yesterday who shaves several times a day, and yet still has all his hair."

"His aim must be terrible," I said.

But of course, that was not what was going on. What explanation did Holmes eventually reveal?

SHRINKING VOCABULARY

"Watson," Holmes once asked me, "do you not fancy yourself to be something of a linguist?"

"Well, not particularly," I replied. "You might say that I dabble, I suppose."

"In that case, I wonder what you make of this linguistic teaser: Can you think of any word that becomes smaller when you add two letters to it?"

"Of course not," I immediately rejoined. "It can't be possible. No word can get smaller when you add letters to it."

But in fact, one could. Which one?

TAKING THE FALL

Holmes came in from the street with his faced flushed from the cold winter air.

"There are a large number of building works on the streets fronting Regent's Park," he informed me. "I'd steer clear of the place, if I were you. It all looks rather unsafe, and in fact I just saw a man fall backwards off a thirty-foot ladder directly onto the stone floor beneath."

"Goodness!" I exclaimed. "Was he alright?"

"Oh yes," said Holmes. "He was completely unharmed."

How was this possible?

The Musgrave Ritual continues from page 179

"He handed me the very paper which I have here, Watson, and this is the strange catechism to which each Musgrave had to submit when he came to man's estate. I will read you the questions and answers as they stand.

"'Whose was it?'

"'His who is gone.'

"'Who shall have it?'

"'He who will come.'

"'Where was the sun?'

"'Over the oak.'

"'Where was the shadow?'

"'Under the elm.'

"'How was it stepped?'

"'North by ten and by ten, east by five and by five, south by two and by two, west by one and by one, and so under.'

"'What shall we give for it?'

"'All that is ours.'

"'Why should we give it?'

"'For the sake of the trust.'

"'The original has no date, but is in the spelling of the middle of the seventeenth century,' remarked Musgrave. 'I am afraid, however, that it can be of little help to you in solving this mystery.'

"'At least,' said I, 'it gives us another mystery, and one which is even more interesting than the first. It may be that the solution of the one may prove to be the solution of the other. You will excuse me, Musgrave, if I say that your butler appears to me to have been a very clever man, and to have had a clearer insight than ten generations of his masters.'

"'I hardly follow you,' said Musgrave. 'The paper seems to me to be of no practical importance.'

"'But to me it seems immensely practical, and I fancy that Brunton took the same view. He had probably seen it before that night on which you caught him.'

"'It is very possible. We took no pains to hide it.'

" 'He simply wished, I should imagine, to refresh his memory upon that last occasion. He had, as I understand, some sort of map or chart which he was comparing with the manuscript, and which he thrust into his pocket when you appeared.'

" 'That is true. But what could he have to do with this old family custom of ours, and what does this rigmarole mean?'

" 'I don't think that we should have much difficulty in determining that,' said I; 'with your permission we will take the first train down to Sussex, and go a little more deeply into the matter upon the spot.'

"The same afternoon saw us both at Hurlstone. Possibly you have seen pictures and read descriptions of the famous old building, so I will confine my account of it to saying that it is built in the shape of an L, the long arm being the more modern portion, and the shorter the ancient nucleus, from which the other had developed. Over the low, heavily-lintelled door, in the centre of this old part, is chiselled the date 1607, but experts are agreed that the beams and stonework are really much older than this. The enormously thick walls and tiny windows of this part had in the last century driven the family into building the new wing, and the old one was used now as a storehouse and a cellar, when it was used at all. A splendid park with fine old timber surrounds the house, and the lake, to which my client had referred, lay close to the avenue, about two hundred yards from the building.

"I was already firmly convinced, Watson, that there were not three separate mysteries here, but one only, and that if I could read the Musgrave Ritual aright I should hold in my hand the clue which would lead me to the truth concerning both the butler Brunton and the maid Howells. To that then I turned all my energies. Why should this servant be so anxious to master this old formula? Evidently because he saw something in it which had escaped all those generations of country squires, and from which he expected some personal advantage. What was it then, and how had it affected his fate?

the story continues on page 202

The Missing Penny

Holmes and I once had a client who refused to meet us in our offices but instead insisted on dining with us at his preferred restaurant. Despite the fact that we were there to help, he made no offer to pay for our meals, so when the bill of thirty pence came, Holmes and I had to pay our share.

Each of us handed ten pence to the waiter. A short while later, however, it transpired that we had been billed incorrectly: we in fact owed only twenty-five pence. On explaining this mistake to us, the waiter proposed that as it would be impossible to perfectly divide the five pence we were owed in return between three, he should give us each one pence back and keep two pence as a tip.

Holmes and I were rather unimpressed by this suggestion, and he later told me of his suspicion that this mistake with the bill was a cheat run by the staff at the restaurant to squeeze extra money out of gullible customers. However, at the time, we did not wish to seem miserly in front of our client, so we politely agreed.

We were all assembling our things and getting ready to leave, when our client suddenly stopped us dead.

"Just a moment!" he exclaimed, making Holmes and myself both jump.

The waiter quickly appeared at his elbow. "Is there a problem, sir?"

"There certainly is! These two gentlemen and I each paid nine pence, making a total of twenty-seven pence. You yourself received two pence. But that adds up to twenty-nine pence. And yet we gave you thirty pence! What happened to the other penny?"

The waiter, looking rather panicked at the prospect of upsetting one of his regular customers, retrieved one of the pennies of his tip and made to hand it back to us.

"That won't be necessary," said Holmes. "The explanation of what has gone on here is quite simple."

What was it?

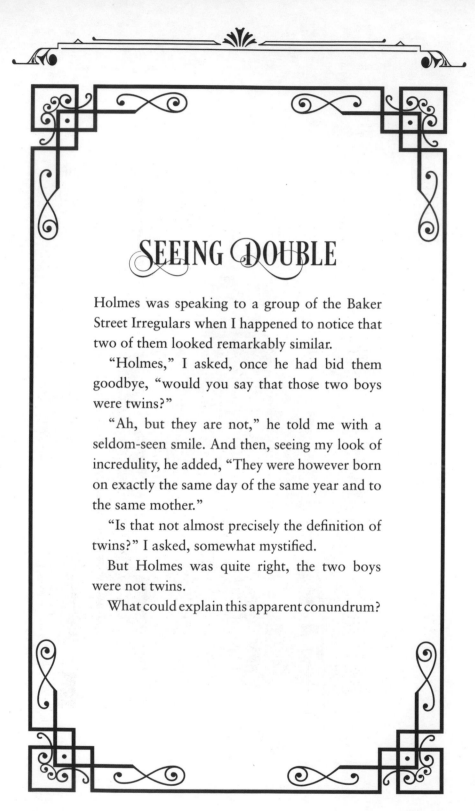

SEEING DOUBLE

Holmes was speaking to a group of the Baker Street Irregulars when I happened to notice that two of them looked remarkably similar.

"Holmes," I asked, once he had bid them goodbye, "would you say that those two boys were twins?"

"Ah, but they are not," he told me with a seldom-seen smile. And then, seeing my look of incredulity, he added, "They were however born on exactly the same day of the same year and to the same mother."

"Is that not almost precisely the definition of twins?" I asked, somewhat mystified.

But Holmes was quite right, the two boys were not twins.

What could explain this apparent conundrum?

THE MANSION MURDER

One Monday in early July, Holmes and I were summoned to a mansion about a half an hour's drive from London. The previous morning, at around eleven o'clock, a shout had been heard in the master bedroom. When the butler went upstairs to investigate he had found the master of the house, Sir Edward Wallingthorpe, lying dead on the floor, strangled by his own scarf.

Holmes and I interviewed everyone at the scene as to their whereabouts at the time of the murder, and each person had a story for us. The cook was in the kitchen, preparing lunch. The maid was in the front hallway, collecting the day's mail. Lady Wallingthorpe was in the drawing room, reading. The butler had been in the dining room, setting the table, before he went upstairs and found the body.

"That hasn't given us much to go on," I said, once we'd finished interviewing them all. "Everyone's alibi is as hard to substantiate as everyone else's. How can we tell who, if any of them, was lying?"

"With ease," said Holmes. "In fact, I'm prepared to instruct an arrest."

Who did Holmes plan to have arrested and why?

MRS. BARKER'S CASE

Holmes and I occasionally received some rather eccentric clients. One in particular who springs to mind is Mrs. Barker, a tiny, trembling woman who arrived at our door clutching a fat, purring tabby cat to her chest. Afraid that she might topple over at any moment I hurried her to a seat, before asking how we could be of service.

"It's B-Bob and S-Sarah," she stammered. "I c-came home to find them lying on the floor, d-dead, absolutely c-covered in glass and water."

At this she dissolved into tears, and we were unable to get another word out of her on the matter. After a rather uncomfortable silence, broken only by Mrs. Barker's sobs, Holmes leaned forward and—changing the subject with uncharacteristic tact—gestured to the cat in Mrs. Barker's lap.

"What is the name of this fine specimen?"

"Mr. T-Tiddles," she replied tearfully.

Holmes reached out and solemnly shook the cat's paw, before turning to me.

"Well, Watson, it seems we have our man."

What had happened to Bob and Sarah?

PINT-SIZED FUN

Holmes and I were having a drink at a local public house one night when a last-minute change of drinks order resulted in the landlord pouring a drink from a half pint to a full pint glass.

"Watson," Holmes said, in that way that demonstrated he had just been inspired by this turn of events. "I've just thought of a rather good problem for you. Imagine that you want to measure out exactly four pints, but you only have two containers, one of which can contain precisely three pints, and the other of which can contain precisely five pints. How do you do it?" He then added, after a short pause, "I should add that you have a beer tap which you can use as much as you wish, and there is no need to worry about wasting some beer en route to your solution."

How could it be done?

An Odd Biography

"I'm reading a book about a rather unusual man, Watson," said Holmes. "He turned thirty in 1740, and yet he was only twenty in 1750."

How could this be?

The Musgrave Ritual continues from page 191

"It was perfectly obvious to me, on reading the ritual, that the measurements must refer to some spot to which the rest of the document alluded, and that if we could find that spot, we should be in a fair way towards finding what the secret was which the old Musgraves had thought it necessary to embalm in so curious a fashion. There were two guides given us to start with, an oak and an elm. As to the oak there could be no question at all. Right in front of the house, upon the left-hand side of the drive, there stood a patriarch among oaks, one of the most magnificent trees that I have ever seen.

"'That was there when your ritual was drawn up,' said I, as we drove past it.

"'It was there at the Norman Conquest in all probability,' he answered. 'It has a girth of twenty-three feet.'

"'Have you any old elms?' I asked.

"'There used to be a very old one over yonder but it was struck by lightning ten years ago, and we cut down the stump.'

"'You can see where it used to be?'

"'Oh, yes.'

"'There are no other elms?'

"'No old ones, but plenty of beeches.'

"'I should like to see where it grew.'

"We had driven up in a dog-cart, and my client led me away at once, without our entering the house, to the scar on the lawn where the elm had stood. It was nearly midway between the oak and the house. My investigation seemed to be progressing.

"'I suppose it is impossible to find out how high the elm was?' I asked.

"'I can give you it at once. It was sixty-four feet.'

"'How do you come to know it?' I asked, in surprise.

"'When my old tutor used to give me an exercise in trigonometry, it always took the shape of measuring heights. When I was a lad I worked out every tree and building in the estate.'

"This was an unexpected piece of luck. My data were coming more quickly than I could have reasonably hoped.

"'Tell me,' I asked, 'did your butler ever ask you such a question?'

"Reginald Musgrave looked at me in astonishment. 'Now that you call it to my mind,' he answered, 'Brunton did ask me about the height of the tree some months ago, in connection with some little argument with the groom.'

"This was excellent news, Watson, for it showed me that I was on the right road. I looked up at the sun. It was low in the heavens, and I calculated that in less than an hour it would lie just above the topmost branches of the old oak. One condition mentioned in the Ritual would then be fulfilled. And the shadow of the elm must mean the farther end of the shadow, otherwise the trunk would have been chosen as the guide. I had, then, to find where the far end of the shadow would fall when the sun was just clear of the oak."

"That must have been difficult, Holmes, when the elm was no longer there."

"Well, at least I knew that if Brunton could do it, I could also. Besides, there was no real difficulty. I went with Musgrave to his study and whittled myself this peg, to which I tied this long string with a knot at each yard. Then I took two lengths of a fishing-rod, which came to just six feet, and I went back with my client to where the elm had been. The sun was just grazing the top of the oak. I fastened the rod on end, marked out the direction of the shadow, and measured it. It was nine feet in length.

"Of course the calculation now was a simple one. If a rod of six feet threw a shadow of nine, a tree of sixty-four feet would throw one of ninety-six, and the line of the one would of course be the line of the other. I measured out the distance, which brought me almost to the wall of the house, and I thrust a peg into the spot. You can imagine my exultation, Watson, when within two inches of my peg I saw a conical depression in the ground. I knew that it was the mark made by Brunton in his measurements, and that I was still upon his trail.

the story continues on page 214

WALKING THE DOGS

Holmes and I were taking a stroll across Regent's Park when we came across a man walking three dogs.

"I'm sure I saw that chap out yesterday with three entirely different dogs," I remarked. "Perhaps people hire him to walk their dogs for them."

"What a strange concept, Watson. But in any case, that gives me an idea for an interesting puzzle," said Holmes. "Let us stipulate that this man has the care of fifteen different dogs, and, moreover, that he is charged with walking each of them every day. He doesn't like walking more than three at once, so he goes on five walks a day with three dogs in tow each time."

"I think I'm with you so far," I said, cautiously. "Where does the puzzle come in?"

"Well, if one found oneself in such a position," Holmes said, "one might naturally wonder whether it would be possible to arrange these walks so that each individual dog is never on a walk with the same dog twice in a week."

"Naturally," I said, somewhat sarcastically. "And what might one naturally conclude on the matter?" I queried.

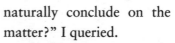

"Well, what do you think, Watson?" replied Holmes.

Could it be done?

THE QUATERNARY SEQUENCE

You will no doubt be pleased to hear, dear reader, that I have only one more of Holmes' sequences to report. This final time we were, I believe, in a restaurant kitchen—a very high-pressure environment in which it is most embarrassing to have a colleague who refuses to speak until you have uttered the required letter, I might add!

The sequence was as follows:

H, T, Q, F, S, S, _

What letter should come next?

BOTTLED UP

After a few drinks at a local hostelry one night, Holmes and I found ourselves with an empty wine bottle. Holmes duly dropped a small coin into the bottle, and then reinserted the cork.

"Say, Watson," he said. "I bet you the next round that I can remove the coin from this bottle without pulling out the cork or breaking the bottle."

Now, although I could see no way of doing it, I was no fool and refused Holmes the bet, knowing full well that he would somehow manage this trick. And indeed I was right.

How did he do it?

Don't Put the Cart Before the Horse

Holmes and I were taking a stroll down a country lane when we came across a most surprising sight. A tree on the right-hand side of the road had been torn from its roots by a recent storm, and had fallen onto a tree on the left-hand side of the road so that it hung across the road. Worse still, a horse and carriage had attempted to pass under the fallen tree but had clearly underestimated how tall the carriage was, and the carriage was now quite perfectly wedged beneath the fallen tree, unable to move either forwards or backwards.

Naturally, Holmes and I went to try and help. Even the combined strength of the two of us and the driver could shift neither the tree nor the carriage, and the driver was in any case loath to risk either damaging the carriage directly, or risk dislodging the tree from its resting place and causing it to crush the carriage.

Luckily, however, Holmes was able to make a very simple suggestion to enable the driver to get his carriage out from under the tree.

What was it?

A Sixth Coded Message

Our sixth coded message was delivered to us at a large mansion, where we were looking into an alleged haunting. The mansion was a short drive from the nearest village, and we believe that it was someone in the village who decided to help us in our investigation. Shortly after finding the shifty-looking note we went outside to find fresh wheel markings on the driveway of the mansion.

Regardless of the identity of the writer, which we never did definitively discover, the contents of the note did eventually prove critical to locating the clever contraption that was responsible for the ghostly goings-on we had been summoned to investigate.

The note read as follows:

MPPL JO UIF
ESBXJOH SPPN

Can you decode the note?
Where did we find the contraption?

AN ENTERTAINING ENIGMA

During a particularly slow afternoon in our chambers, Holmes and I had rejoined for a hot beverage when he chose to spring another of his unexpected riddles on me.

"Here's a little puzzle to keep your brain sharp on this dullest of days, Watson," he said, with something of a twinkle in his eye. "The riddle is this: It enters dry, and yet comes out wet. The longer it's in, the stronger it gets. What is it?"

CROSSING THE THAMES

"I witnessed an entertaining sight, today, Watson," Holmes informed me. "Two boys—friends, I believe—both wished to cross the Thames. They had only a single one-person boat between them. Yet they both managed to cross in the boat, without either of them having to swim, and without them using any sort of trick to get the boat across without any occupants."

How was this possible?

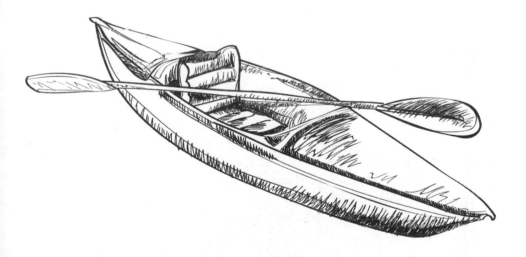

The Musgrave Ritual continues from page 203

"From this starting-point I proceeded to step, having first taken the cardinal points by my pocket-compass. Ten steps with each foot took me along parallel with the wall of the house, and again I marked my spot with a peg. Then I carefully paced off five to the east and two to the south. It brought me to the very threshold of the old door. Two steps to the west meant now that I was to go two paces down the stone-flagged passage, and this was the place indicated by the Ritual.

"Never have I felt such a cold chill of disappointment, Watson. For a moment it seemed to me that there must be some radical mistake in my calculations. The setting sun shone full upon the passage floor, and I could see that the old, foot-worn grey stones with which it was paved were firmly cemented together, and had certainly not been moved for many a long year. Brunton had not been at work here. I tapped upon the floor, but it sounded the same all over, and there was no sign of any crack or crevice. But, fortunately, Musgrave, who had begun to appreciate the meaning of my proceedings, and who was now as excited as myself, took out his manuscript to check my calculation.

"'And under,' he cried. 'You have omitted the "and under".'

"I had thought that it meant that we were to dig, but now, of course, I saw at once that I was wrong. 'There is a cellar under this then?' I cried.

"'Yes, and as old as the house. Down here, through this door.'

"We went down a winding stone stair, and my companion, striking a match, lit a large lantern which stood on a barrel in the corner. In an instant it was obvious that we had at last come upon the true place, and that we had not been the only people to visit the spot recently.

"It had been used for the storage of wood, but the billets, which had evidently been littered over the floor, were now piled at the sides, so as to leave a clear space in the middle. In this space lay a large and heavy flagstone with a rusted iron ring in the centre to which a thick shepherd's-check muffler was attached.

"'By Jove!' cried my client. 'That's Brunton's muffler. I have seen it on him, and could swear to it. What has the villain been doing here?'

"At my suggestion a couple of the county police were summoned to be present, and I then endeavoured to raise the stone by pulling on the cravat. I could only move it slightly, and it was with the aid of one of the constables that I succeeded at last in carrying it to one side. A black hole yawned beneath into which we all peered, while Musgrave, kneeling at the side, pushed down the lantern.

"A small chamber about seven feet deep and four feet square lay open to us. At one side of this was a squat, brass-bound wooden box, the lid of which was hinged upwards, with this curious old-fashioned key projecting from the lock. It was furred outside by a thick layer of dust, and damp and worms had eaten through the wood, so that a crop of livid fungi was growing on the inside of it. Several discs of metal, old coins apparently, such as I hold here, were scattered over the bottom of the box, but it contained nothing else.

"At the moment, however, we had no thought for the old chest, for our eyes were riveted upon that which crouched beside it. It was the figure of a man, clad in a suit of black, who squatted down upon his hams with his forehead sunk upon the edge of the box and his two arms thrown out on each side of it. The attitude had drawn all the stagnant blood to the face, and no man could have recognized that distorted liver-coloured countenance; but his height, his dress, and his hair were all sufficient to show my client, when we had drawn the body up, that it was indeed his missing butler. He had been dead some days, but there was no wound or bruise upon his person to show how he had met his dreadful end. When his body had been carried from the cellar we found ourselves still confronted with a problem which was almost as formidable as that with which we had started.

"I confess that so far, Watson, I had been disappointed in my investigation. I had reckoned upon solving the matter when once I had found the place referred to in the Ritual; but now I was there, and was apparently as far as ever from knowing what it was which the family had concealed with such elaborate precautions. It is true that I had thrown a light upon the fate of Brunton, but now I had to ascertain how that fate had come upon him, and what part had been played in the matter by the woman who had disappeared. I sat down upon a keg in the corner and thought the whole matter carefully over.

the story continues on page 226

CRUMBLED UP

Holmes and I came home to find that, seized by a rare fit of enthusiasm for baking, Mrs. Hudson had decided to attempt to make some plum crumble. As we arrived, however, she was in a state of despair.

"Whatever has happened, Mrs. Hudson?" I asked her. "Is there anything we can do to help?"

"Not unless you can turn back time," she replied. "I've put all the plums in but I wasn't counting how many, and now it turns out that the amount of sugar you need to add is proportional to the number of plums. It's ruined! And they were such nice plums too."

"I'm sure it's not too important," I assured her. "A rough estimate will do."

"No need for that," said Holmes. "Mrs. Hudson, I believe we can determine exactly how many plums you put in the crumble."

What strategy did he have in mind?

A LONG YEAR

"And how old are you?" I asked Mrs. Hudson's youngest great nephew.

"I'll be turning seven next year!" he told me, flushed with pride and keen, as children so often are, to seem older than they really are.

"And to think," said his older sister, "that he was only four years old the day before yesterday."

Is it possible that both of their statements are true?

THE ONE RULE

I was sitting down to dinner with Holmes one night when he suddenly removed the salt from the table.

"Watson, I'm imposing a rule on you, until such time as you determine what that rule is."

I sighed, but did not bother protesting.

"You are allowed pepper, but not salt. You are allowed beef but no lamb. Carrots, yes, cabbage and broccoli if you so desire, but no potato, in any form. Oh, and you must eat with a spoon."

What was the rule?

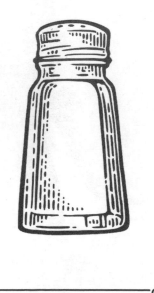

KEEPING CLEAN

Holmes and I were consulting with a couple of the Baker Street Irregulars when a sudden gust of wind picked up some dirt from the ground and blew it towards their faces, covering one boy's face in dirt and yet somehow leaving the other's completely clean. But strangely enough, it was the boy with the clean face who ran to a nearby water barrel to wash his face, while the other remained where he was.

I turned to Holmes with a quizzically raised eyebrow but, as usual, Holmes was unsurprised.

What explanation did Holmes provide?

The Three Children

Holmes once had a visit from an old acquaintance whom I had never met before. I found them chatting freely in a way he seldom did with me as I came in to offer them some tea.

"And how are your children?" Holmes was asking. "You have three, if I remember rightly, although I must admit I don't quite recall their ages."

"You always enjoyed deduction, didn't you, old chap?" his acquaintance replied. "What if I told you that the product of their ages was 40?"

"That's not quite enough information for me to deduce their ages," said Holmes.

"Alright, well I shall add that the sum of their ages is the number of years we've known each other."

Holmes considered this. "I'll still need a tad more."

"Finally, the youngest was our first summer baby, born in July."

"Ah, I see."

Holmes suddenly turned to me. "Why don't you tell this gentleman the ages of his children, then, Watson?"

I balked. "But I don't know how long you've known each other!"

"That doesn't matter, Watson! You now have enough information to deduce it."

And indeed I did. How old are the three children?

The Family Name

"I ran into an old acquaintance today, Watson," Holmes informed me, as we sat at the dinner table.

"That's always a pleasant surprise," I replied. "Had it been a long time since you had last seen one another?"

"Quite," Holmes replied. "It was in fact closing in on fifteen years."

"Goodness, why that's almost half a lifetime," I exclaimed.

"A whole lifetime, for some," said Holmes, rather sadly. "In any case, as it turns out my friend had married ten years ago, to someone I have never met, and today I was introduced to their eight-year-old daughter."

"How sweet," I said. "What was her name?"

"I asked the girl the same thing and, as is typical of children, she didn't give me a plain answer. Instead she told me it was the same as her mother's, and of course that was enough."

"How was that enough to establish her name, if you have never met her mother?"

"My dear Watson," Holmes exclaimed, "I believe you've made another one of your fallacious inferences."

What was my mistake?

THE FOURTH REBUS

One morning, Holmes failed to make his usual curmudgeonly appearance at the breakfast table. He had worked late into the night, so I did not want to risk awakening his acerbic wrath by knocking on his bedroom door to query as to whether anything was the matter. But as morning became afternoon, however, I began to worry, so I tentatively tapped on the frame of his door. He said nothing that I heard, but a folded piece of paper soon pushed itself out from under his door.

It read:

What was he communicating?

AN UNCRACKABLE SEQUENCE

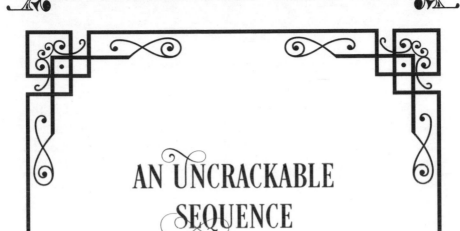

Sitting down to wait for Holmes in his office one day, my eye strayed across a piece of paper with one of his infernal sequences on it. This one was made up of numbers, which read as follows: 16 06 68 88. Feeling certain that he had left it there on purpose to vex me, I set about trying to work out what could possibly link the numbers, but in truth I sat there for a good half an hour and yet still the answer eluded me.

Finally, Holmes came in, and saw me struggling.

"Go on then, Holmes," I said to him. "Put me out of my misery. What's the connection here?"

Holmes laughed. "Why, Watson, it's the very simplest of sequences."

And once he told me, I saw that he was right. What connected the numbers?

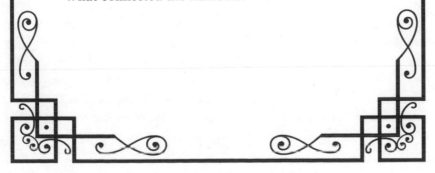

The Musgrave Ritual continues from page 215

"You know my methods in such cases, Watson. I put myself in the man's place and, having first gauged his intelligence, I try to imagine how I should myself have proceeded under the same circumstances. In this case the matter was simplified by Brunton's intelligence being quite first-rate, so that it was unnecessary to make any allowance for the personal equation, as the astronomers have dubbed it. He knew that something valuable was concealed. He had spotted the place. He found that the stone which covered it was just too heavy for a man to move unaided. What would he do next? He could not get help from outside, even if he had someone whom he could trust, without the unbarring of doors and considerable risk of detection. It was better, if he could, to have his helpmate inside the house. But whom could he ask? This girl had been devoted to him. A man always finds it hard to realize that he may have finally lost a woman's love, however badly he may have treated her. He would try by a few attentions to make his peace with the girl Howells, and then would engage her as his accomplice. Together they would come at night to the cellar, and their united force would suffice to raise the stone. So far I could follow their actions as if I had actually seen them.

"But for two of them, and one a woman, it must have been heavy work the raising of that stone. A burly Sussex policeman and I had found it no light job. What would they do to assist them? Probably what I should have done myself. I rose and examined carefully the different billets of wood which were scattered round the floor. Almost at once I came upon what I expected. One piece, about three feet in length, had a very marked indentation at one end, while several were flattened at the sides as if they had been compressed by some considerable weight. Evidently, as they had dragged the stone up they had thrust the chunks of wood into the chink, until at last, when the opening was large enough to crawl through, they would hold it open by a billet placed lengthwise, which might very well become indented at the lower end, since the whole weight of the stone would press it down on to the edge of this other slab. So far I was still on safe ground.

"And now how was I to proceed to reconstruct this midnight drama? Clearly, only one could fit into the hole, and that one was Brunton. The girl must have waited above. Brunton then unlocked the box, handed up the contents presumably—since they were not to be found—and then—and then what happened?

"What smouldering fire of vengeance had suddenly sprung into flame in this passionate Celtic woman's soul when she saw the man who had wronged her—wronged her, perhaps, far more than we suspected—in her power? Was it a chance that the wood had slipped, and that the stone had shut Brunton into what had become his sepulchre? Had she only been guilty of silence as to his fate? Or had some sudden blow from her hand dashed the support away and sent the slab crashing down into its place? Be that as it might, I seemed to see that woman's figure still clutching at her treasure trove and flying wildly up the winding stair, with her ears ringing perhaps with the muffled screams from behind her and with the drumming of frenzied hands against the slab of stone which was choking her faithless lover's life out.

"Here was the secret of her blanched face, her shaken nerves, her peals of hysterical laughter on the next morning. But what had been in the box? What had she done with that? Of course, it must have been the old metal and pebbles which my client had dragged from the mere. She had thrown them in there at the first opportunity to remove the last trace of her crime.

"For twenty minutes I had sat motionless, thinking the matter out. Musgrave still stood with a very pale face, swinging his lantern and peering down into the hole.

"'These are coins of Charles I,' said he, holding out the few which had been in the box; 'you see we were right in fixing our date for the Ritual.'

"'We may find something else of Charles I,' I cried, as the probable meaning of the first two questions of the Ritual broke suddenly upon me. 'Let me see the contents of the bag which you fished from the mere.'

the story continues on page 238

A PRIESTLY POSER

Holmes and I once tackled a case that involved the disappearance of a priest, and at one point our investigations brought us to a remote hilltop chapel.

"Watson," Holmes said, as we began our ascent up the broad stone steps, "consider this. A priest sets off at nine a.m. up a path to a hilltop chapel, and arrives at nine p.m. The following day, he sets off at nine a.m., and reaches the bottom at nine p.m. Is there any moment on the second day at which he is at exactly the same step on the path at exactly the same time as he was on the previous day?"

I frowned. "Surely that depends on his speed, and whether he took breaks at any point on either day," I answered. "How can you possibly know the answer without more information?"

"Know?" he replied. "I can do one better. I can prove it."

What was Holmes' proof?

THE LONG THROW

Holmes found an old tennis ball of mine lying about our chambers, which I presume prompted him to put the following challenge to me: "Watson, how would you throw this ball as hard as you can so that, without bouncing it off anything or it being caught and returned by anyone, it is certain to always come straight back to you?"

How was I to do it?

A SEVENTH CODED MESSAGE

The seventh coded message we received concerned a client of ours named Mr. Alexander. Mr. Alexander ran a restaurant in a well-to-do part of the city, but he came to us because he had noticed that his figures weren't adding up: someone was stealing money as it made its way from the tables to the cash repository.

In his employment were seven people: Frank Pale, the chef; Martin Heal, the head waiter; Janet Bars, a waitress; Richard, Charlie, and Mark Sharp, the bussers; and David Pound, the sommelier. Any one of them could be the thief.

It was midway through our investigation that we received the following anonymous tip-off:

HE SARP BRS PAL
ALEXNDER'S POUND.
-THOMAS

We asked Mr. Alexander if he knew anyone called Thomas, and he told us he did not. But curiously it was this very fact that led Holmes to crack the code.

Who was responsible for the missing money?

RUNNING IN CIRCLES

"Watson," Holmes said to me one day as we were walking down Baker Street, "have you ever noticed that removable manhole covers are almost always circular in shape?"

"I must say I'd never really thought about it," I replied, "but now you point it out I can see that it's true."

"I suppose," said Holmes somewhat pensively, "that if you reflect on the matter for a moment it turns out to be not in the least surprising."

What reason did Holmes see for removable manhole covers needing to be round rather than square or rectangular?

THE FIFTH REBUS

A Miss Juliet Williams had sought out Holmes' services to help retrieve some valuable jewels which had apparently vanished from her locked cabinet. A little investigation had led us to suspect her brother-in-law, and we were beginning to close in on him when she received the following message in the post from her brother-in-law:

What did it say?

The Long Corridor

"How about a little breakfast brainteaser?" Holmes asked me the other morning, peering out from behind his newspaper.

I knew better than to bother protesting, so I waited for him to continue.

"There is a corridor lined with one hundred doors. One hundred people are waiting at one end. The first person goes through the corridor and opens every door. The second goes through and shuts every second door. The third changes every third door—shutting it if it's open, and opening it if it's shut. The fourth changes every fourth door, the fifth every fifth, and so on, right up until the one hundredth person, who only changes the very last door. Given all of this activity, can you say which doors will be open at the end of this process?"

Sighing, I reached for my pen and began marking out the doors on my own newspaper, so as to work my way through them one by one.

"No, no, Watson," Holmes said, waving his hand dismissively at me. "There's no need for copious note-taking. The answer is really very simple when you consider the question properly."

Can you see what Holmes meant?

DEARLY BELOVED

"I met a man the other day who has married over a hundred women," Holmes announced to me one day.

"Well that's clearly entirely inappropriate!" I replied. "After a certain number of divorces, surely one must realize that one is not the marrying kind."

"Oh, but on the contrary, my dear Watson, the man has never divorced, and all the women are quite happy."

What perfectly logical explanation was Holmes able to offer for this? The man was not, I might add, a polygamist.

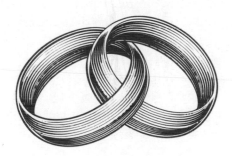

The *Musgrave Ritual* continues from page 227

"We ascended to his study, and he laid the debris before me. I could understand his regarding it as of small importance when I looked at it, for the metal was almost black and the stones lustreless and dull. I rubbed one of them on my sleeve, however, and it glowed afterwards like a spark in the dark hollow of my hand. The metal work was in the form of a double ring, but it had been bent and twisted out of its original shape.

"'You must bear in mind,' said I, 'that the royal party made head in England even after the death of the king, and that when they at last fled they probably left many of their most precious possessions buried behind them, with the intention of returning for them in more peaceful times.'

"'My ancestor, Sir Ralph Musgrave, was a prominent Cavalier and the right-hand man of Charles II in his wanderings,' said my friend.

"'Ah, indeed!' I answered. 'Well now, I think that really should give us the last link that we wanted. I must congratulate you on coming into the possession, though in rather a tragic manner of a relic which is of great intrinsic value, but of even greater importance as an historical curiosity.'

"'What is it, then?' he gasped in astonishment.

"'It is nothing less than the ancient crown of the kings of England.'

"'The crown!'

"'Precisely. Consider what the Ritual says: How does it run? "Whose was it?" "His who is gone." That was after the execution of Charles. Then, "Who shall have it?" "He who will come." That was Charles II, whose advent was already foreseen. There can, I think, be no doubt that this battered and shapeless diadem once encircled the brows of the royal Stuarts.'

"'And how came it in the pond?'

"'Ah, that is a question that will take some time to answer.' And with that I sketched out to him the whole long chain of surmise and of proof which I had constructed. The twilight had closed in and the moon was shining brightly in the sky before my narrative was finished.

"'And how was it then that Charles did not get his crown when he returned?' asked Musgrave, pushing back the relic into its linen bag.

"'Ah, there you lay your finger upon the one point which we shall probably never be able to clear up. It is likely that the Musgrave who held the secret died in the interval, and by some oversight left this guide to his descendant without explaining the meaning of it. From that day to this it has been handed down from father to son, until at last it came within reach of a man who tore its secret out of it and lost his life in the venture.'

"And that's the story of the Musgrave Ritual, Watson. They have the crown down at Hurlstone—though they had some legal bother and a considerable sum to pay before they were allowed to retain it. I am sure that if you mentioned my name they would be happy to show it to you. Of the woman nothing was ever heard, and the probability is that she got away out of England and carried herself and the memory of her crime to some land beyond the seas."

The Treacherous Trap

Holmes and I received a message from Inspector Lestrade concerning a recent murder that had taken place in West London. George Anderson had been found dead in his apartment in Hammersmith, and the police had reason to believe the murderer was extremely dangerous, so they told us they were sending an armed escort to take us to the crime scene.

When the doorbell eventually rang, we were greeted by a heavily built young man with a large nose and thick eyebrows. We got into a carriage with him and were driven out west to Hammersmith. I have to say I was a little nervous about the whole affair, but I had insisted on accompanying Holmes, so I was sure not to let on.

When we arrived, our police escort produced a key and unlocked the front door. Behind it was a small hallway with several doors opening off it, and a narrow flight of stairs at the end.

"This way," he said, gesturing to the distant staircase. "The body's on the upstairs floor, not down here."

At these words Holmes froze, and turned to me. "Watson," he said very quietly, "I believe this is a trap. Let us try to retreat without him noticing."

We managed to escape, and it did transpire that the man who had shown us to the house had not been sent by the police. But how did Holmes know?

SOLUTIONS

The First Deduction 8

Tom was the boy with bushy hair, and had worked on The Case of the Vanishing Glass. Mickey was the boy with the scar under his eye, and had worked on The Crimson Consideration, while Joe was the boy with the mole on his chin, and had worked on The Mark of Three.

A Special Number 12

It's the only number which contains all ten digits in alphabetical order.

The Fast Train 13

The train to Leicester leaves two minutes earlier than the train to Dover. There are therefore only two minutes out of every twenty during which the Dover train is the next to leave, or in other words, the Dover train is only the next to leave ten per cent of the time.

The Case of the Red Widow 14

The Earl had looked up to see the woman framed brightly in sunlight through the doorway, in front of the whitewashed wall. As he blinked, she happened to walk away, leaving him with the bright inverse afterglow that appears whenever you have looked at a brightly lit object. Against the whitewashed wall, he saw the glowing complementary hue of her dress, turning the vivid green into a brilliant, shining red.

The Impossible Breakfast 15

Lunch and dinner.

Four By Four 16

There are multiple possibilities for some numbers but there is at least one way of making every number from 1 to 20:

$$1 = \frac{4}{4} \times \frac{4}{4}$$

$$2 = \frac{4}{4} + \frac{4}{4}$$

$$3 = \frac{4+4+4}{4}$$

$$4 = 4 + 4 \ (4 - 4)$$

$$5 = \frac{(4 \times 4) + 4}{4}$$

$$6 = \frac{4!}{4} \times \frac{4}{4}$$

$$7 = (4 + 4) - \frac{4}{4}$$

$$8 = 4(\frac{4+4}{4})$$

$$9 = \frac{4}{4} + 4 + 4$$

$$10 = (\frac{4}{\sqrt{4}}) + (4 \times \sqrt{4})$$

$$11 = (\frac{(4! \times \sqrt{4}) - 4}{4})$$

$$12 = 4(4 - \frac{4}{4})$$

$$13 = (\frac{(4! \times \sqrt{4}) + 4}{4})$$

$$14 = 4 \times (\sqrt{4} + \sqrt{4}) - \sqrt{4}$$

$$15 = (4 \times 4) - \frac{4}{4}$$

$$16 = (4 \times 4) + 4 - 4$$

$$17 = (4 \times 4) + \frac{4}{4}$$

$$18 = (4 \times 4) + 4 - \sqrt{4}$$

$$19 = 4! - (4 + \frac{4}{4})$$

$$20 = 4 \times (4 + \frac{4}{4})$$

SOLUTIONS

The Present-Packing Poser 17

Yes—I could pack the parcels in the following way:
Crate one: 15 pound parcel and 10 pound parcel.
Crate two: 13 pound parcel, 11 pound parcel, and 1 pound parcel.
Crate three: 9 pound parcel, 8 pound parcel, 4 pound parcel and two 2 pound parcels.

A Mysterious Place 18

A map.

Great Nieces and Great Nephews 20

This rule would not change the biological probability of having a girl from being 50 per
cent, so would not affect the gender ratio. It would simply affect how many children a
particular couple might have.

The Barrel Quarrel 24

Holmes removed the lid of the barrel and then tipped the barrel so the beer was level with
the lowest part of the top of the barrel. As the bottom of the barrel was not at all visible
when he did this, they could be sure that the landlord was right: the barrel was more than
half full. Had some of the bottom of the barrel been visible, this would have vindicated the
customer instead.

Brothers and Sisters 25

They both have four children.

Reading Room 26

He simply read only during daylight hours.

The Three Feet Feat 27

A yardstick.

A First Keyboard Conundrum 28

Somewhat aptly, TYPEWRITER is one of the longest words you can type. It is not alone
among ten-letter words, however, since PERPETUITY, PREREQUIRE, PROPRIETOR,
and REPERTOIRE are also possible.

Keeping Up With The Hudsons 29

Mrs. Hudson's sister is 60. (Her children are 40, 37, 34, and 31.)

The Cuboid Calendar 30

Yes, it was possible. To create every number from 1 to 31, you need the following
twelve digits: 0, 1, 1, 2, 2, 3, 4, 5, 6, 7, 8, 9, which as you will see fit perfectly onto the
twelve faces of two cubes. There must be a 1 and a 2 on each cube, and the 0 and the
3 must be on different cubes.

SOLUTIONS

6,210,001,000

I was to send the box to Holmes with my padlock on it. When he received it, he could then attach a padlock of his own to the box and send it back. When I then received it, I could then unlock my original lock and send it back to him with only his own padlock on it.

The quickest possible time (ignoring time taken to switch/flip rashers) is three minutes. This can be achieved by frying slices 1 and 2 on one side for one minute, then removing 1, flipping 2 and frying 3 for one minute (so 2 is now done on both sides), and then frying the other side of 1 and 3 for one minute.

Agatha and Beatrice are Mrs. Hudson's nieces, and Jane and Margaret are Agatha's daughters (and therefore Mrs. Hudson's great nieces).

The next letter is U. The sequence is first letters of planets in the solar system, starting with the closest to the sun and moving outwards.

The probability is 1/33. This is obtained from dividing the probability that both are twos ($4/52 \times 3/51 = 12/(51 \times 52)$) by the probability that one is a two ($396/(51 \times 52)$).

The best strategy is to put a single red apple into one of the sacks and the rest of the apples in the other sack. That way, one sack gives a 100% chance of picking a red apple and the other gives a 48.7% chance; overall, this is a 74.3% chance of getting a red apple.

One of the apples you give away can be given while still in the sack.

He walked to Paris, Texas, not Paris, France.

A caterpillar has no wings, but will one day be able to fly when it becomes a moth or butterfly.

SOLUTIONS

The First Rebus..51

Back ache.

The Impatient Pocket Watch................................52

It was twenty-four minutes past one. When it is actually 1pm, Watson's watch shows 2:40pm. And when it is actually 2pm, Watson's watch shows 3:45pm. Currently the watch shows 3:06pm, which means the real time is sometime between 1pm and 2pm. To calculate the number of minutes past the hour, note that they are 26 minutes into the 65 minute 'hour' shown by the watch. Because the watch runs 5 minutes fast per hour, this means that every 12 minutes of real time the watch advances 13 minutes. So these 26 left-over minutes on the watch correspond to 2x13 minutes of watch time, or 2x12 minutes of real-time. Therefore the time is 1:24pm.

Celebrity Conundrum.......................................54

Surnames.

The Third Deduction.......................................57

In The Adventure of the Broken Table, Sarah Doyle was robbed by Peter Watkins. In The Adventure of the Frozen Lake, Mark Robinson was murdered by Charlotte Green. In The Adventure of the Moving Statue, John Bell was defrauded by Juliet Lane.

Lost and Found...60

Wherever you find something is always the last place you look because once you've found it, you simply stop looking!

The Second Keyboard Conundrum............................61

The longest commonly used words are ALASKA, FLASKS, SALADS, and SALSAS. Longer than those are ALFALFAS, plants in the pea family, and HAGGADAH, a Jewish text.

Crossing The Bridge.......................................62

This is possible in seventeen minutes. First, Holmes and Lestrade cross over, which takes two minutes. Then Lestrade goes back with the torch, taking another two minutes. Next, Mrs. Hudson and I cross, which takes ten minutes. Then Holmes goes back with the torch, taking another minute, and finally, Holmes and Lestrade cross over for the final time, taking another two minutes. This brings the total time to seventeen minutes.

Juggling Juices...64

I simply need to pour the contents of the second glass into the fifth glass and then return the second glass to its original position.

SOLUTIONS

Cake Conundrum 66
There were fourteen slices of cake on the children's plate.

A Coded Message. 68
COME TO FIFTEEN JUNIPER STREET. The spaces between the words have been changed, and unnecessary line breaks added.

The Mixed-Up Label. 69
Mrs. Hudson should take a spoonful from the jar labelled "MIXED". If she tastes sugar, she will know that this was the jar of pure sugar, meaning the jar labelled "SALT' must be the mixed jar and the jar labelled "SUGAR" must be the salt jar. If she tastes salt, she would likewise know that this was the jar of pure salt, meaning the jar labelled "SALT' must be the sugar jar and the jar labelled "SUGAR" must be the mixed jar.

Another Card Conundrum 72
Yes, it does make a difference. In the first case, as you may recall, the probability is 1/33, whereas in the second case, when we know it's a two of hearts specifically, the probability is 1/17, obtained from dividing the probability that both are twos and one is the two of hearts (6/(51x52)) by the probability that one is the two of hearts ((51+51)/(51x52)). In other words, in the second case, the probability of drawing two twos is almost twice as high. Knowing that one of the cards is a two of hearts, rather than just any two, narrows down the number of possible combinations in which both cards are a two, since combinations such as the two of diamonds and the two of spades are ruled out. What's more, it narrows down the number of possible combinations in which it is not the case that both cards are twos, since combinations such as the two of diamonds and the three of diamonds are then ruled out. So, knowing that you have a two of hearts gives you a much better chance of getting two twos than just knowing you have a two.

The Two Dentists 74
Given that there are only two dentists in the town, we can assume that they are each other's dentists. In this case, the dentist with the better teeth can be inferred to be the worse dentist, since he will be treated by the other dentist.

The Circular Puzzle 75
The words that Holmes found are cede, cited, deceit, deceive, detect, device, dice, die, diet, dive, edict, edit, evicted, iced, teed, tide, tied, vetted, and vied, plus the nine-letter word "detective".

The Secondary Sequence. 77
The next letter is S. The sequence consists of the first letters of days of the week, starting from Tuesday.

SOLUTIONS

The book was stolen by Nicholas Richardson, since it can be deduced he was the third person to visit the archives. As the old man says, the book was still there for the entirety of the second person's visit.

Holmes had added sugar to his tea before he saw the fly. As soon as he tasted the "new" cup, he could tell it was the same one, because it already had sugar in it.

The subscription for *The Needlepoint Nut* works out to be much cheaper than that of *The Fowl Fanatic*, even after one year but certainly after four.

There was one rose, one tulip and one geranium.

All of these words have their letters in alphabetical order.

The trick is to realize that the coins can be put on top of each other, and not just flat on the table. Once you realize this, you can place three coins flat on the table, each one touching the other two in a triangular formation, and then put the fourth on top of them.

The Clock Tower is 105 yards tall.

Including the two I spoke to, there were a total of four sisters and three brothers.

The man was in the uniform of a hansom cab driver and so was clearly a driver, but at that time he wasn't actually driving—he was simply walking.

He's under arrest. (HEs under a rest)

Magnets. The box appeared to get much heavier when on a metal table, which could be caused by the contents of the box being magnetically attracted to the table.

SOLUTIONS

The Door Dilemma

Ask the guard whether the other guard would say that this is the right door. If it is the right door, then either guard will answer "no". If it is the wrong door, then either guard will answer "yes".

The Cake Trios

I could eat all three cakes from the largest tin, and then place the smallest tin inside the now empty largest one. This way, each tin would still contain three cakes.

The Scone Problem

I said to Holmes, "You will not give me a plain or a raisin scone." Holmes could not then give me nothing, as that would make my statement true, nor could he give me a plain or raisin scone, as that would make my statement false: his only remaining option was to give me the chocolate chip scone I desired.

Wet Clothes

10 ounces. One per cent of 20 is 0.2, so the clothes on their own must weigh 0.2 ounces. If 0.2 ounces make up two per cent of the overall weight, the overall weight must be 10 ounces.

The Slow Workmen

Four men.

A Second Coded Message

In the basement of 9 Camden Road. The message has its 'A's swapped with its 'E's and its 'I's swapped with its 'O's. The decoded message thus reads: THE ARTWORK YOU SEEK IS IN THE BASEMENT OF NINE CAMDEN ROAD.

An Odd Order

They were standing back to back.

The Fifth Deduction

Red was shipping diamonds from the East storehouse on Monday. Yellow was shipping rubies from the South storehouse on Tuesday. Blue was shipping emeralds from the North storehouse on Wednesday. Green was shipping sapphires from the West storehouse on Thursday.

Sleeping It Off

If the husband died on the spot, he wouldn't have been able to report his dream to anyone.

SOLUTIONS

Getting the Chop...................113
Meat. I am still unclear whether this was a joke on Holmes' part or a genuine misunderstanding: both seem equally unlikely.

The Case of the Secret Sailors...................114
The password was WELCOME. The clocks on the wall represented flag semaphore characters spelling out this word.

Irregular Twins...................116
The day was the 29th of February. If the twins were born on either side of midnight of the 28th of February, on a non-leap year, then on a leap year their birthdays would be two days apart.

A Puddle Puzzle...................120
A towel.

The Tertiary Sequence...................121
The next letter is R. The sequence consists of the last letters of months of the year.

The Strange Shipwreck...................122
As they are survivors, they won't be buried at all. Or at least not any time soon, hopefully.

A Palindromic Puzzle...................124
The next palindromic number would be 25,052, which is 110 more than 24,942.

Racing Results...................125
If a dog in second place is overtaken, the dog overtaking is now in second place, not first place.
If a dog is in last place then a dog overtaking it must have lapped the others, and it could be in any position other than last.

Carnival Cakes...................126
The actual weight of the cake was 72 ounces, meaning that my guess was the closest, and Holmes admitted I had beaten him for perhaps the only time in my life.

Matching Socks...................127
Taking seven socks would ensure at least three matching pairs. Even if Watson picked out seven socks of the same shade then he would have three matching pairs (and one extra).

SOLUTIONS

The twelve-letter word (re-using letters) is COCKLESHELLS. A few eleven-letter ones are CHROMOSOMES, HORSESHOERS, REMORSELESS, SCHOOLROOMS, and SORCERESSES. The nine-letter word is HORSESHOE.

All of these words can be either a noun or a verb, and are pronounced differently in each case.

I needed to turn the first switch on for a few minutes and then turn it off again. I was then to turn the second switch on and leave the third off. After that, I was to go down into the cellar. If the light was on, I would know it was the second switch that lit the cellar. If the light was off, I should then feel the bulb. If it was warm then I would know that it had recently been on, and was therefore controlled by the first switch. If not, it must be controlled by the third switch.

A key.

Yes, he should. There are two scenarios: either the woman is a Truth-teller or she is a Liar. If she is a Truth-teller, then the right-hand side of the conditional—"I am a Truth-teller"—is true, so she will go to dinner.
Alternatively, if the woman is a Liar, then the right-hand side of the conditional—"I am a Truth-teller"—is false and she says she will not go to dinner, but we know she is lying so in fact she will go to dinner.
Either way, it is true that she will go to dinner with him.

The poison was in the ice in the punch. When the Colonel drank his glass of punch the ice hadn't yet melted, but later in the party it did, which was when the poison was released into the punch and those who drank it were poisoned.

It was to inform us that Mark knew who did it. The question mark was intended to read as the words "Question Mark", giving: QUESTION MARK: HE KNOWS WHO DID IT.

The two opposite sides of a die always add up to seven. So Holmes merely needed to add seven to the total he could see in front of him to get my overall total.

SOLUTIONS

It was driven over in winter, when the lake was frozen over.

A pillow.

ROGERS BROTHER STRANGLED PROFESSOR BURNS. All but the first and last letter of each word have been put in reverse order.

My best bet is to choose the lions. If they haven't been fed for five weeks they are almost certainly dead, and if not then they must be very weak!

A complete set of dominoes will join together to form a complete ring. By secretly removing a piece before the children started joining them, Holmes was able to guarantee that the numbers at either end of the line were the same as those on the removed piece.

A book's pages are numbered starting from the right-hand side, meaning that page 48 would be on the back of page 47 and nothing could be between them.

Holmes' thought was that the cake could be sliced into four using two cuts from top to bottom, in the usual way, and then cut a third time across the middle, halving each of the initial four slices.

The dealer should deal from the bottom of the pack and go around counterclockwise, starting with himself.

As the taller of the two of us, Holmes has the longer arms, so was able to reach higher than I could have done.

Page 28 is on the same sheet as pages 9, 10, and 27.

SOLUTIONS

Truth-tellers and Liars Two 163

He should claim to be a poor Liar. This means he cannot be a poor Liar, or he would be telling the truth. He also cannot be a Truth-teller, since he would then be telling the truth and she does not want him to be a Truth-teller. So, of the available options, he must be a rich Liar.

A Fair Race 164

The taller boy would still win. The first race demonstrated that the taller boy could run 50 yards in the time it took the shorter boy to run 45 yards. So if the taller boy started five yards behind, they would draw level five yards from the end of the race, the taller boy having run 50 yards and the shorter 45 yards. As the taller boy is faster, he would run the final five yards more quickly, and win the race.

A Banana Bargain 168

Apples are normally 2 pence each, bananas 4 pence, and oranges 8 pence, so the total cost for one of each would be 14 pence.

Target Practice 169

The first bullet would be shot immediately, not after ten seconds. So in a minute, at a rate of ten seconds per shot, he should manage seven shots.

The Broken Five 170

60 times. Note that it's easy to count 55, 155, 255 as one digit when there are two in each.

The Tricky Testimony 172

If the witness had only seen the attacker from behind, he would not have been able to see the paint on the front of his dungarees. So the witness must have either lied in his testimony or already known in some other way that the attacker had paint on the front of his dungarees.

Tying the Knot 174

For a man to have a widow, he must be dead. Therefore he is quite incapable of marriage.

A Table Tennis Trick 175

Holmes filled the crack with water. This caused the air-filled ball to rise to the top, where we could easily pick it up.

The Cube Quandary 176

There are ten possible combinations: a) zero blue faces, b) zero red faces, c) one blue face, d) one red face, e) two blue faces that are adjacent, f) two blue faces that are opposite each other, g) two red faces that are adjacent, h) two red faces that are

SOLUTIONS

opposite each other, i) three red faces that all share one vertex, and j) three red faces, two of which are opposite each other.

If the Petri dish is half full at 11.30 a.m., then it will be completely full when all the bacteria divide in two a minute later, at 11.31 a.m.

A carpet.

Lucian Atkins. The name was spelled out by the first letter of every word in the message.

It is certainly possible to predict the future—it's getting it right that's the difficult part!

We just needed to retrieve the marker and turn it so the place we'd just come from was correctly indicated. The other destinations would then also be correctly indicated.

Scrambled eggs.

The man was a barber.

The word "small" becomes "smaller" when you add "er" to the end.

He had been on the bottom rung of the ladder when he fell.

The initial figure of thirty pence is irrelevant to the transaction. In actual fact, the two pence given to the waiter is not something extra on top of the twenty-seven pence paid, but is rather the difference between the twenty-seven pence paid and the corrected twenty-five pence bill.

Seeing Double 194

The two boys were not twins but rather triplets.

The Mansion Murder 197

Holmes planned to arrest the maid. She claimed to be collecting the mail, but the murder happened on a Sunday, so there would not have been any mail to collect.

Mrs. Barker's Case 198

Bob and Sarah were goldfish, and Mr. Tiddles had pushed their bowl onto the floor.

Pint-sized Fun. 200

Start by filling the five-pint container, and then pouring it into the three-pint container, thus leaving two pints in the five-pint container. Next, empty the three-pint container and pour the two pints from the five-pint container into it. Then completely fill the five-pint container again, and pour this quantity into the three-pint container until it is full. You will be left with exactly four pints in the five-pint container.

An Odd Biography 201

The man was born in 1770 BC.

Walking the Dogs 204

It can certainly be done. Identifying the fifteen dogs as A to O, here is one such arrangement:

Monday	Tuesday	Wednesday	Thursday	Friday	Saturday	Sunday
A-F-K	A-B-E	B-C-F	E-F-I	C-E-K	E-G-M	K-M-D
B-G-L	C-D-G	D-E-H	G-H-K	D-F-L	F-H-N	L-N-E
C-H-M	H-I-L	I-J-M	L-M-A	G-I-O	I-K-B	O-B-H
D-I-N	J-K-N	K-L-O	N-O-C	H-J-A	J-L-C	A-C-I
E-J-O	M-O-F	N-A-G	B-D-J	M-N-B	O-A-D	F-G-J

The Quaternary Sequence. 206

The next letter is E. The sequence consists of the first letters of fractions with increasing denominators: half (1/2), third (1/3), quarter (1/4), fifth (1/5), and so on.

Bottled Up. 207

Holmes pushed the cork into the bottle. He was then able to tip out the coin.

Don't Put the Cart Before the Horse 208

Holmes suggested that the man release the air from the wheels of his carriage in order to reduce its height and allow it to be freed from the tree.

SOLUTIONS

In the drawing room. The message was encoded by shifting every letter by one letter alphabetically. The decoded message read: LOOK IN THE DRAWING ROOM.

Tea.

The boys began on opposite sides of the Thames.

Holmes suggested counting the stones of the plums, which, of course, had not been added to the crumble.

Yes, if the statements were made on the 1st January, and the boy's birthday was the previous day. That way, he could have been four on the 30th December, turned five on the 31st December, be due to turn six on the 31st December of the current year, and due to turn seven on the 31st December of the next year.

I was only allowed items containing the same letter repeated consecutively.

The boy with the clean face saw the boy with the dirty face and assumed his own face was dirty too, whereas the boy with the dirty face saw the boy with the clean face and made the opposite assumption.

The children are 1, 5, and 8. Given that Holmes couldn't deduce their ages despite knowing the sum of their ages, I could have worked out that the sum of their ages was 14. This is because from all the possible combinations that would yield the product of 40, only two have the same sum: 1, 5, 8, and 2, 2, 10. The final clue was necessary to choose between these two options. If two of the children were 2, then they would have to be twins. The final clue rules out this possibility.

The friend Holmes ran into was the girl's mother.

He had a splitting headache.

SOLUTIONS

An Uncrackable Sequence

I was looking at the piece of paper upside down. It in fact read: 88 89 90 91.

A Priestly Poser

Imagine there are two priests both setting off at nine a.m.: one from the top of the path and one from the bottom. For them to both reach the other end of the path at nine p.m., they must cross each other at some point. The necessity of this crossing proves that the priest from Holmes' question must have at some point been in the same place at the same time on the second day as he was on the first.

The Long Throw

I needed to throw the ball straight up vertically into the air.

A Seventh Coded Message

The Sharp Brothers. The word THOMAS indicates the letters missing from the words in the main message, and their position. So a T is the first letter of the first word, and H the second letter of the second word, and so on. The decoded message reads: THE SHARP BROS PALM ALEXANDER'S POUNDS.

Running in Circles

A round manhole cover cannot fall into the hole, whereas a square or a rectangular one could. It may also be noted that a circular manhole cover can be easily rolled, which could facilitate moving it.

The Fifth Rebus

Forgive and forget.

The Long Corridor

The open doors would be doors 1, 4, 9, 16, 25, 36, 49, 64, 81 and 100, or in other words, the square-numbered doors. This is because these are the only numbers with an odd number of factors, so they are changed by an odd number of people and end up being left open.

Dearly Beloved

The man was a priest.

The Treacherous Trap

We were supposed to be taken to the crime scene, which was the apartment where George Anderson was murdered. The place to which we were taken was clearly a multi-floor residence, and therefore could not have been the flat.